"Over the years I have come to value so much the unusual gifting of Paul Chilcote as a Wesleyan scholar and author. He has the rare ability to share the rich treasures of his own faith tradition both with those of his own tribe and beyond. This he always does in a way that is fresh, winsome, and powerfully attractive. In *Praying in the Spirit of Christ* he accomplishes this again. Here he takes the rich devotional inheritance that shaped the lives of the Wesley brothers, drills down deep and makes it available to us in 52 prayers that we can pray ourselves. Phrased in contemporary English, Paul shows how an 'ancient-future' approach to discipleship can speak so powerfully to our hearts and minds today. You can be sure that as you live with this book, you will be drawn into the kind of faith that works through love towards a holiness of heart and life. I commend this work highly and with much gratitude to God for Paul's life and witness."

—Trevor Hudson, author of *Discover Your Spiritual Identity*

*Praying in the Spirit of Christ*

# *Praying in the Spirit of Christ*

52 Devotions for Today

PAUL W. CHILCOTE

CASCADE *Books* • Eugene, Oregon

PRAYING IN THE SPIRIT OF CHRIST
52 Devotions for Today

Copyright © 2017 Paul W. Chilcote. All rights reserved. Except for brief quotations in critical publications or reviews, no part of this book may be reproduced in any manner without prior written permission from the publisher. Write: Permissions, Wipf and Stock Publishers, 199 W. 8th Ave., Suite 3, Eugene, OR 97401.

Cascade Books
An Imprint of Wipf and Stock Publishers
199 W. 8th Ave., Suite 3
Eugene, OR 97401

www.wipfandstock.com

PAPERBACK ISBN: 978-1-5326-1180-3
HARDCOVER ISBN: 978-1-5326-1182-7
EBOOK ISBN: 978-1-5326-1181-0

*Cataloguing-in-Publication data:*

Chilcote, Paul Wesley, 1954–.

Praying in the spirit of Christ : 52 devotions for today / Paul W. Chilcote.

Description: Eugene, OR : Cascade Books, 2017 | Includes bibliographical references and index.

Identifiers: ISBN 978-1-5326-1180-3 (paperback) | ISBN 978-1-5326-1182-7 (hardcover) | ISBN 978-1-5326-1181-0 (ebook)

Subjects: LCSH: Wesley, John, 1703–1791. | Wesley, Charles, 1707–1788. | Methodist Church—Prayers and devotions—English.

Classification: BX8337 .C48 2017 (print) | BX8337 .C48 (ebook)

Scripture taken from the Common English Bible®, CEB® Copyright © 2010, 2011 by Common English Bible.™ Used by permission. All rights reserved worldwide. The "CEB" and "Common English Bible" trademarks are registered in the United States Patent and Trademark Office by Common English Bible. Use of either trademark requires the permission of Common English Bible.

Manufactured in the U.S.A.                                        OCTOBER 11, 2017

In memory of my father,
Virgil Chilcote,
who taught me to appreciate
the legacy of the saints

# Contents

*Preface xi*
*Introduction xiii*
*Suggestions for Using These Devotions xix*

1. The Gifts of God  1
2. The Mysterious Way  4
3. True Christianity  7
4. Christian Witness  10
5. Genuine Peace  13
6. Faith Working through Love  16
7. The Great Commandment  19
8. The Incarnation  22
9. The Intercession of Christ  25
10. A Spirit of Power  28
11. Growing in Love  31
12. God Is Gracious  34
13. The Presence of God  37
14. The Light of Christ  40
15. God's Commandments  43
16. Love Divine  46
17. The Desire of the Heart  49
18. Give Thanks  52
19. Pray Continually  55
20. The Altar of the Heart  58
21. The Face of God  61
22. Humility  64
23. This Holy Mystery  67
24. Communion with God  70
25. God's Providential Care  73
26. Follow the Spirit  76

CONTENTS

27. The Gospel Feast  79
28. The Sacred Meal  82
29. The Weight of Sin  85
30. Arise, Shine  88
31. Our Daily Labor  91
32. Our Refuge and Strength  94
33. The Saints' Rest  97
34. A Clear Conscience  100
35. Doers of the Word  103
36. Patience in Suffering  106
37. Seek the Lord  109
38. Practicing the Presence  112
39. Heart Religion  115
40. Genuine Spirituality  118
41. Liberty in Christ  121
42. Resurrection Joy  124
43. The Glorious King  128
44. Love Your Enemies  131
45. Servants of God  134
46. The Cross of Christ  137
47. The Work of Christ  140
48. Breathing God's Love  143
49. Thirst for God  146
50. A Fellowship of Love  149
51. Perfect Love  152
52. Pure, Unbounded Love  155

*Contemporary Editions of Original Sources*  159
*Scripture Index of Devotion Texts*  161
*Index of Hymns*  163

# Preface

A number of years ago I published a devotional book entitled *Praying in the Wesleyan Spirit*. In that volume I "translated" John Wesley's so-called "standard sermons" into the forms of prayer in order to make them more accessible to the contemporary reader. Over the course of the intervening years I have been gratified by so many communications I have received from readers who found that book to be helpful in their Christian walk. People who used that resource shared with me the way in which the prayers, hymns, and scripture texts opened a new world of grace, hope, and love to them and enriched their lives as Christian disciples.

I have often thought about producing a volume parallel to that book, but only recently received inspiration for the book that you are now reading. In 1755 John Wesley completed his publication of a *Christian Library*, a collection of some of his favorite devotional and theological writings. He wanted to make these classical texts available to the rank and file of the early Methodist movement and beyond. It struck me that this collection would be an amazing resource for the contemporary Christian, but it was so huge—fifty volumes! My idea, therefore, was to identify one work from each volume (or so), select a manageable excerpt from Wesley's extract, translate it into the form of a prayer, and modernize it for the contemporary ear and sensibility. This, then, is precisely what I have done here. This book will expose you to what John Wesley considered to be vital devotional material in the Christian heritage—insights from spiritual mentors that helped him understand the faith better and live as a Christian more faithfully. These selections provide a panoramic view of the *Christian Library*. They are, therefore, a collection of great Christian works that is simultaneously broad and deep. I have identified each of the sources for the readings and have also indicated in brackets which volume of Wesley's *Christian Library* it appeared in originally.

The purpose of this book is not academic. This is not a scholarly resource. I have made no effort to produce a precisely accurate edition of the

## Preface

original texts, even as edited by Wesley. My primary purpose has been to capture the spirit of the original authors in winsome contemporary forms of prayer. I have provided a scripture passage for each selection. This locates the topic within the larger world of the biblical witness. In many, if not all of these excerpts, the authors actually identify the biblical reference point, either explicitly or implicitly. So your journey through these devotional materials will carry you through the fertile soil of God's Word as well.

In addition to the biblical texts and the prayers, I have also included relevant excerpts from the amazing hymns of Charles, John, or Samuel Wesley for each section. All of these hymns may be found in *The United Methodist Hymnal (UMH)*. While many of them will be well-known to you, I assume that others will be new, perhaps never even sung. One of the great saints of the early church said that to sing is to pray twice. So sing these hymns—at least in your heart if not out loud. Each of the hymn selections is intentionally keyed to the texts and themes of the prayers. Hopefully, the inclusion of these hymn texts will enable the Spirit to touch your life in a different way than the prayers themselves.

In the editorial work I have done on the prayers I have been very intentional in my use of inclusive language. Given the fact that many of the sources are seventeenth century or earlier, this has presented untold challenges. The hymns of Charles Wesley also present hurdles of their own in this regard. I made the decision, therefore, to retain the language as presented in *The United Methodist Hymnal* since careful editors attended to this issue when the hymnal was in preparation during the 1980s. I always want to be inclusive. My hope is that, in those selections where masculine language had to be retained for one reason or another, this does not create a barrier to anyone who seeks to meet God in these readings.

I pray that you will engage this rich treasury of Christian devotion by reading it, pondering it, singing it, and then, hopefully, by putting it into practice. The Wesleyan way of living the Christian faith is dynamic and profoundly relational. It is a process of faith working by love leading to holiness of heart and life. Invite the Holy Spirit to be your companion as you journey through these devotions. The Spirit breathed life into the original authors and the Spirit longs to breathe new life into you as you open yourself to the spiritual insight and wisdom of these mentors in the faith. Permit the Spirit to shape you through those rich resources that shaped the lives of the Wesleys and the early Methodist people.

Paul Chilcote<br>
Feast of St. Francis of Assisi, 2016

# Introduction

John Wesley (1703–91) conceived the Christian life as *via devotio*—a way of devotion. Despite the fact that he called himself a "man of one book," he was one of the most well-read people of his day. He focused much of his reading in the devotional classics of the Christian heritage. He drank deeply from the well of Christian spirituality and the material he imbibed shaped his life in profound ways. His life reflected what he read. Charles Wesley (1707–88) viewed the Christian life as *via cantorum*—a way of singing. Without question, scripture functioned as the primary source for his nine thousand hymns, but he also incorporated ideas, themes, and images from the many Christian writers who had shaped his life. Since the early Methodist people learned their theology by singing it, the breadth and depth of Charles's sources shaped the robust character of the doctrine and spirituality they lived.

It is always important to remember that Methodism—the movement birthed by the Wesleys—was a movement of renewal within the Church of England. The paradigm for the renewal of the church that the Wesley brothers embraced reflects an "ancient-future" approach. They reached back into the fertile history of the church, and particularly to the great Christian mentors of the previous two centuries, in order to envisage an unfolding future filled with hope. They felt a close connection to the great cloud of witnesses, to the apostles and martyrs and saints that preceded them in faith over the centuries. They learned from their writings, borrowed their practices, received inspiration from their stories, and took courage from their witness. Their approach reflected the comprehensive—*via media* or middle way—vision of their Anglican heritage. This fundamental orientation provided a perennial reminder to them that the family of God—a truly catholic or universal church—is always much larger than any of us can imagine. As a consequence of this expansive vision, John and Charles

*Introduction*

developed a broad, deep, long, and high conception of Christian faith and practice.

They loved the primitive church and learned from sainted figures like Macarius, Irenaeus, and Clement of Alexandria. Works like Thomas à Kempis's *Imitation of Christ*, Blaise Pascal's *Thoughts*, and Brother Lawrence's *Practice of the Presence of God*—all examples of a Roman Catholic spiritual tradition—shaped John and Charles's practical mysticism. The reformers and theologians of their own Anglican heritage—men like Thomas Cranmer, Richard Hooker, and later, Jeremy Taylor—rooted them in the magisterial tradition of Protestantism. They appreciated the simplicity for which the English Puritans longed and the holiness of life, or purity, exemplified by mentors like John Bunyan, Thomas Goodwin, and Joseph Alleine. From the Pietists Johann Arndt and Auguste Hermann Franke they learned about the importance of a religion of the heart. The salient themes that emerged as a consequence of diverse influences such as these include the foundation of the grace and love of God, the way of salvation, accountable discipleship in a community of grace, and compassionate mission in God's world.

Above all, John and Charles Wesley preached and sang a "practical divinity." Not so much concerned about "speculative theology," their primary concern was to promote a gospel that touched people where they really lived. They sought to inspire their followers by the example of others who lived as the children God created them to be. Their vision of life in Christ was ancient, biblical, practical, and timely. It should be no surprise, then, that their teachings and writings remain vital, dynamic, meaningful, and relevant today.

In 1749 John Wesley began work on his monumental *Christian Library: Consisting of Extracts from, and Abridgments of, the choicest Pieces of practical Divinity which have been published in the English Tongue in Fifty Volumes*. When he brought this project to completion in 1755, this collection amounted to no less than fourteen thousand pages of devotional and theological material culled, edited, and "improved" from more than a hundred authors spanning fifteen centuries. Since the meditative selections in this book are all drawn from this extensive library, it will be helpful to provide some background about the purpose and the contents of this collection.

As the Methodist movement gained momentum in the 1740s, John Wesley was particularly concerned about providing spiritual guidance for the burgeoning number of his followers in the structured Societies (and particularly their leaders) and to facilitate spiritual growth among them all. Many of the early Methodists were uneducated. The growing army of itinerant preachers under his oversight lacked formal theological training. Other movements on the English religious landscape at that time espoused different views of salvation—truncated understandings of the gospel, in John and Charles's view—that could easily pervert the dynamic gospel of faith working by love they preached and sang. John and Charles wanted to educate those in their movement and to provide the kind of resources they needed to stay on track in their new-found faith. Wesley's preachers had particular need in this regard and the *Christian Library* was most certainly intended primarily for them. Indeed, John declared it required reading for them all! This library, he thought, could help his preachers and people abide in Christ and grow in grace, and would expand their vision of the Christian walk.

The *Christian Library* was not the only large collection he published, although it was his most ambitious project. Just several years before he began work on this collection, in fact, he published a library of theological treatises in fifteen volumes—*Wesley's Tracts* (1746)—containing no less than sixty-five items of which more than half were his own. Later in life he published his collected works in thirty-two volumes (1771–74), including carefully selected material from his *Journal*, letters, sermons, and other writings. Begun in 1778, the *Arminian Magazine* included material from four different arenas: doctrinal treatises, biographies and autobiographies, letters to and from Wesley, and poetry. Another collection, published jointly by both brothers, has particular significance, as it functioned as a parallel of sorts to the *Christian Library*. A descriptive phrase in the Preface to *A Collection of Hymns, for the Use of the People Called Methodists*, published in 1780, denotes the parallelism. It describes the 560 hymns as "a little body of experimental and practical divinity." Like the *Christian Library*, its primary purpose revolved around practical divinity, providing an account of scriptural Christianity, declaring the grandeur of religion, cautioning against error, and affording directions on how to live a holy life.

On March 25, 1749, John Wesley prepared the preface for the *Christian Library* at his famous Kingswood School in Bristol. He identifies four of his primary hopes with regard to this collection. First, he hoped that "serious readers" might gain the most for their lives by reading fine examples of practical divinity. Second, he hoped that the *Library* might facilitate the possibility of spiritual transformation in the lives of Methodists. Third, he hoped that a review of the materials, organized in chronological

*Introduction*

order, might convince the reader that primitive Christianity is the common thread that connects all the authors from beginning to end. Fourth, and perhaps most importantly, he hoped that God would use the *Library* to shape the hearts of Methodists and others. He concludes the Preface, therefore, with a prayer to this effect: "May the Giver of every good gift, give it his blessing, and write his love in every reader's heart!"

The contents of the collection may be divided rather neatly into several categories with regard to the sources: patristic writers, foreign authors (German, French, and Spanish), anonymous materials, Church of England theologians, and Puritan authors. The student of John Wesley, knowing how significant the influence of the early church had been upon him, will be struck by the dearth of patristic sources—only four: Clement of Rome, Polycarp, Ignatius, and Macarius. He includes five translations of non-English material from extremely significant, and primarily Roman Catholic, devotional writers and twenty-nine Anglican authors, primarily from the so-called Caroline Divines, participants in a golden age of Anglican scholarship and devotional writing during the reigns of Charles I, and after the Restoration, Charles II. Thomas Ken and Jeremy Taylor stand out as exemplars of this high church tradition. Somewhat surprising is the inclusion of excerpts from the writings of no less than thirty-one English Puritans, whose religious heritage stands in stark contrast to the Anglican authors and, even more so, to the Arminian theology of the Wesleys. Even more shocking, with regard to the "lives" (or biographical sketches) included in the collection, Puritan examples outnumber the Anglicans thirty-six to eight.

Several comments are appropriate with regard to this "Puritan presence" in the *Christian Library*. It is important to remember that both Samuel and Susanna Wesley, the parents of the sons, were born and raised in Puritan homes. The boys, therefore, inherited a deep and abiding appreciation for the Puritan emphasis on scripture, simplicity, and particularly sanctity. While the Wesley home combined an Anglican desire to please God in all things and a Puritan sense of abiding in God, the themes of abiding and growing in grace dominate the collection. One of the greatest threats to the Wesleyan way at this time was an attitude known as antinomianism—the view that faith made effort and growth superfluous in the Christian life. So Wesley selected the literary works of Puritan writers that best instructed Methodists with regard to growing in grace and persevering in holiness. Moreover, in order to help his itinerant preachers in this regard with practical advice, he carefully selected biographies of Puritans from

# INTRODUCTION

the sixteenth and seventeenth centuries that illustrated a life of piety based on conscience and a continual striving after purity in the Christian life. He hoped that his followers would learn thereby, not to be almost only, but altogether Christians.

In the same way that John Wesley gathered prose material—his own as well as others—which he then published in collections, Charles produced many collections of hymns over the course of his lifetime. The most well-known of these were the various editions of *Hymns and Sacred Poems* that he published between 1739 and 1749. But he also published collections on the Lord's Supper, on the great festivals of the Christian Year, and on the Trinity, as well as other themes and topics. The most impressive of all these collections was that of 1780 already noted as a parallel to the *Christian Library*. The vast majority of the Wesley hymns in these collections grew out of the questions asked by real people in real time attempting to live out their life of faith in real ways. The major themes of his hymns correspond, as one might expect, with the primary tenets of Wesleyan theology: the all sufficiency of God's grace, holiness of heart and life, and the proclamation of God's love and their counterparts related to the identity of all people as the children of God, the integration of Christian faith with practice, and the inclusive character of Christian community. Early Methodists sang these themes at the outset of the revival and this practice remains a hallmark of the tradition.

*The United Methodist Hymnal (UMH)* includes fifty-nine hymns written or translated by John, Charles, and Samuel Wesley, their father, drawn from twenty different eighteenth-century collections. The diversity and broad spectrum of the hymns included in this hymnal immediately strikes the singer. John Wesley's translations of German hymns, like "Thou hidden love of God" by Gerhard Tersteegen, are some of the earliest published Methodist hymns included in the *UMH*. The only Samuel Wesley text included in the *UMH*, "Behold the Savior of mankind," was printed originally with the German hymns in *A Collection of Psalms and Hymns* in 1737, the first English hymnbook printed in North America. Charles Wesley originally composed "Whether the Word be preached or read" in 1783, a hymn never published in a hymnbook or collection during his lifetime. So the Wesley hymns in the *UMH* span the years 1739 to 1783.

The Wesleys published the vast majority of these hymns (31) in the four *Hymns and Sacred Poems* collections between 1739 and 1749. Two other substantial collections, generally styled *Redemption Hymns* (1747) and *Scripture Hymns* (1762), also figure prominently in the *UMH*. Hymns

## INTRODUCTION

from most of Wesley's collections for the great Christian festivals like Christmas, Easter, and Pentecost are represented in the *UMH*, along with other significant hymns from collections like *Hymns on the Lord's Supper* (1745). Forty-nine of the fifty-nine Wesley hymns in the *UMH* are included here in conjunction with the fifty-two devotions. Stanzas of three hymns—"Maker, in whom we move," "Jesu, thy boundless love to me," and "Love divine, all loves excelling"—are used for more than one devotion, but without repeating any verses. This amazing collection of hymns, in and of itself, merits serious reflection and contemplation alongside the prayers and biblical texts that make up this devotional book.

The selections from the *Christian Library* included in this volume, drawn from such a wide range of Christian devotional literature, are an important legacy of the Methodist tradition. Hardly anyone today even knows about John Wesley's *Christian Library*, a resource that helped shape the lives of the early Methodist people. These readings, along with the hymn selections that accompany them here, represent a rich treasury of spiritual insight. Wesley prayed that God would write the love of Christ on the hearts of those who read and meditated on this material. That is why he published his fifty-volume collection. He wanted the people of his own day to experience God's love, to be transformed by it, and to grow into the most loving people they could be in this life. My hope is that you will make Wesley's prayer your own as you read, ponder, and put these devotions into practice. May God write love on your heart.

## Suggestions for Using These Devotions

There are a number of ways you can use this resource. Perhaps the most obvious way is to center each successive week of the year on each of the readings in turn. You may read the selection on Sunday, at the beginning of the week, or read it daily throughout the course of the week. In this way you will immerse yourself through the course of a full year in selections from devotional classics that John Wesley held in high esteem and put into the hands of his Methodist people. You may actually be inspired to obtain some of the works from which these extracts are drawn for future devotional exercises. I have provided some recommendations in this regard in the "Original Sources" index at the back of this volume.

You may also use these meditations at the beginning and ending of each day. If you were to pray selections one and two on the first day, three and four on the second, and so forth, through fifty-two, you would be able to make your way through the entire collection in the course of a month (actually twenty-six days with Sundays left out for other religious practices and corporate worship). The liturgical seasons of Advent and Lent would be particularly appropriate times for this approach.

Yet another option would be to read the meditations in their entirety, straight through. Following this practice, you obtain the "big picture," so to speak, in one sitting. This enables you to get an immediate sense of the major themes, primary concerns, and full range of images related to the Christian life. To have a sense of the whole is often very helpful. But since these are devotions, and not a simple narrative, they are really intended for a more contemplative pace of reading. Time for reflection—allowing the devotions to sink into your spirit—is also important. A day apart, or a day long retreat, might provide the opportunity to read through this material in a more leisurely and spiritually uplifting way.

You may want some basic instruction on how to meditate on these devotions. One of the most classic forms of meditation is known as *lectio*

## Suggestions for Using These Devotions

*divina.* Literally meaning "divine reading," this spiritual practice cultivates the ability to listen and permits the Spirit to shape your response in thought, prayer, and action. Most Christians conceive this practice as four movements: *lectio* (reading), *oratio* (prayer), *meditatio* (meditation), and *contemplatio* (contemplation). In your reflection on each selection, you simply move successively through each of these steps. Permit me to simplify this meditative technique by orienting what you do around the four simple words *proclaim, picture, ponder,* and *practice.* I will make this very practical.

- *Proclaim.* Read the selection for the day. You may even consider reading it out loud. This might be particularly helpful if you use this in a group.
- *Picture.* Read the same text through again. This need not be done immediately. You may be steeping yourself in one of the fifty-two readings over the course of a full week. So whenever you read the text for the second time, move to this next phase. Essentially, ask yourself the question, where do I fit into this?
- *Ponder.* After a third reading of the text, ponder what these words might mean for you today. What insight have you gained about yourself, God, your neighbor? What significance do you attach to your discoveries given your recent experiences, relationships, concerns?
- *Practice.* Following a final reading of the selection, resolve to translate your experience of the devotion into action. What is God calling you to do with this today? What action is required?

Using this four-step meditative technique might enhance your experience of God through these readings and bring greater meaning to the scripture and hymns as well.

In a separate appendix I have provided a listing of the scriptural texts associated with each devotion in their canonical order. You may prefer to read through these selections in the order of the texts, giving attention to and time for meditation upon each of the passages. Note the amazing range and diversity of texts around which the readings revolve. There is great breadth and depth here.

On the basis of reports from those who have used *Praying in the Wesleyan Spirit,* I highly recommend that you use this book in groups. Sharing a journey through this material in a group—prayer groups, covenant discipleship groups, Bible studies, class meetings—multiplies insight and enhances the benefit to your spirit. If you are a pastor, feel free to use this material in Sunday or midweek worship experiences where you can provide others an opportunity to sink their buckets into this deep well of spiritual insight from Christian mentors of the past. Be attentive to the Spirit's voice as you read these classic texts. Most assuredly, you can find wonderful material here for sermons and Sunday School classes!

Open yourself to the leading of the Spirit. However you choose to use this book, approach the experience prayerfully. Ask God to speak to you through the insights of these great devotional writers. You may even want to begin each reading with the simple prayer: "Lord, you speak to me through your Word, the hymns of the church, and words from the great cloud of witnesses. Open my heart to hear your voice through these words today." Once you have pondered their words, the scripture text, and the Wesley hymns that "sing the theme" for each devotion, seek to live out God's vision in your daily life. As God makes faith effective through love in this way you will experience God's transforming power in your lives more fully.

# 1

## *The Gifts of God*

**Scripture:**

All things are from him and through him and for him. May the glory be
to him forever. Amen.

—Romans 11:36

**Prayer:**

Your gifts, O God, are so blessed, wonderful, and beloved.
    You offer us the gifts of life and immortality, righteousness and glory,
        truth and honesty, faith and confidence, temperance and
            holiness!
    How can we even begin to imagine all you have prepared
        for those who wait upon you?
We yearn so deeply, O God, to be found in the number of those who wait
    for you,
    that we may be partakers of these blessed and wonderful gifts.
    We seek those things that are pleasing and acceptable to you.

## Praying in the Spirit of Christ

> We desire to align our lives with your will and follow the way of truth.
> You lavish your gifts upon us so freely.
> We come to know just how blessed we are, O God, when we fix our eye upon Christ:
> > Through Christ we behold your glorious face, as in a mirror;
> > Through Christ the eyes of our hearts are opened;
> > Through Christ our darkened understanding rejoices in your marvelous light.
> We yearn to be safe in Christ, O God, through and through.
> > Help us, then, to live in such a way that
> > > we never despise the weak,
> > > we share the abundance of our blessings with the poor,
> > > we demonstrate our wisdom, not in words, but in good works.
> > > we live in humility without bringing attention to ourselves.
> Having received all these things from you, O God, we give you thanks,
> > to whom be glory for ever and ever. Amen.

—Clement of Rome, *1 Corinthians 1:35–40* [1]

**Hymn:**

Praise the Lord who reigns above
    and keeps his court below;
praise the holy God of love
    and all his greatness show;
praise him for his noble deeds,
    praise him for his matchless power;
him from whom all good proceeds
    let earth and heaven adore.

God, in whom they move and live,
    let every creature sing,

glory to their Maker give,
    and homage to their King.
Hallowed be thy name beneath,
    as in heaven on earth adored;
praise the Lord in every breath,
    let all things praise the Lord.

*—UMH* 96:1, 3

# 2

## *The Mysterious Way*

**Scripture:**

Jesus answered, "I am the way, the truth, and the life. No one comes to the Father except through me."

—John 14:6

**Prayer:**

It is hard for me to imagine sometimes, O God, just how precious I am in your sight;
> that I am your friend—the spouse of the heavenly Bridegroom.
> But because of your love, I am able to know the true worth of my soul,
>> and I can ponder the mysteries of your loving presence.
> It remains a great mystery to me but, by the glory of your transcendent light,
>> I also see my own fallen and broken condition.
> I understand that I am called to suffer with Jesus,
>> to be crucified with him so that I might rise again with him,
>> and forever reign together with him.

This mysterious life in Christ, O God, sometimes overwhelms me.
    You declare my nobility; you call me to royal dignity.
        You proclaim that I am your beloved child.
    The glory of an earthly king and his riches perish and fade away;
        but the kingdom and riches of our Lord and Christ
            are eternal, heavenly and glorious,
                incorruptible and never passing away.
    You describe me as a co-heir with Christ and promise to me
        those things that no eye has seen, or ear has heard,
            or that haven't crossed the mind of any human being.
    You offer the Comforter to me—you desire to fill me with your loving Spirit;
        and so, I am filled with unquenchable desire for you.
I wholeheartedly embrace the pilgrimage of life in you, O God, and in the midst of it all
    I discover what it means to be a true follower of Christ;
        I celebrate the victory that is mine in him.
    Help me to travel the road of life with great patience,
    in hope, in humility, in poverty of spirit, and in gentleness,
        for I know that these are the signposts that mark the royal way,
            leading all who travel this road to the heavenly city.
Glory be to the tender mercies of the Father,
    and of the Son, and of the Holy Ghost, forever! Amen.

                —Macarius of Egypt, *Homilies*, 27 [1]

**Hymn:**

Come, thou long expected Jesus,
    born to set thy people free;
from our fears and sins release us,
    let us find our rest in thee.
Israel's strength and consolation,
    hope of all the earth thou art;

## Praying in the Spirit of Christ

dear desire of every nation,
   joy of every longing heart.

Born thy people to deliver,
   born a child and yet a King,
born to reign in us forever,
   now thy gracious kingdom bring.
By thine own eternal spirit
   rule in all our hearts alone;
by thine all sufficient merit,
   raise us to thy glorious throne.
—*UMH* 196

# 3

## *True Christianity*

**Scripture:**

So then, if anyone is in Christ, that person is part of the new creation. The old things have gone away, and look, new things have arrived!

—2 Corinthians 5:17

**Prayer:**

To be a true Christian, O God, is to have your image stamped upon my soul,
    shining through all the actions of my life.
    It is the righteousness and holiness of truth.
        It is your very life indwelling me.
To be a true Christian, O God, is an active, lively, strong, vigorous principle,
    seated in the inmost soul and shaping all the thoughts, words,
        and actions that emanate from a life centered in you.

Lord I want to be a true Christian.
>   I want my life with you to be a vital heat, an inward flame.
>   I want everything that proceeds from my faith
>> to be free, ready, loving, steady, uniform, and unconstrained.
> Shape me into a true Christian so that
>> I will be content in all things, watchful and self-controlled,
>>> always imitating Christ, with everything I say and do
>>>> emanating from an inward principle of grace.
> Love is the true characteristic and peculiar badge of Christianity.
>> Nothing is stronger than love.
> So fill me with this spirit of love
>> and the myriad of graces that flow from it.
>>> Love is your royal law, and wherever you plant it,
>>>> it takes hold and flourishes.
>> Wherever it flourishes, it reflects your beauty.

To be a true Christian, O God, means to have your love established in my heart
> —this heart of your child, O God,
>> So let it shape every area of my life.
> May your love turn every thought, every desire, every action,
>> and every inclination of my mind into a sacrifice of praise to you. Amen.

—Johann Arndt, *True Christianity (Part 1, Introduction)* [1]

**Hymn:**

Jesu, Thy boundless love to me
  no thought can reach, no tongue declare;
O knit my thankful heart to thee
  and reign without a rival there.

Thine wholly, thine alone, I am;
   be thou alone my constant flame.
O grant that nothing in my soul
   may dwell, but thy pure love alone!

O may thy love possess me whole,
   my joy, my treasure, and my crown.
Strange flames far from my soul remove,
   my every act, word, thought, be love.

*—UMH* 183:1–2

# 4

## Christian Witness

**Scripture:**

The righteousness that I have comes from knowing Christ, the power of his resurrection, and the participation in his sufferings.

—Philippians 3:10

**Prayer:**

You are the only health of all people, O God,
    and the everlasting life of those who die in you.
        I submit myself wholly unto your blessed will.
            Since nothing can perish that is committed unto your mercy,
                I move toward death in sure hope that
                      you will restore my life again at the last,
                          in the resurrection of the just.
Strengthen me against all temptations, O God.
    and defend me with the belt of your mercy.
        I acknowledge that in myself there is no good hope of salvation.
            All my confidence, hope, and trust are in your most merciful
                goodness.

I have no merits or good works which I may claim before you.
> You, merciful Lord, were born for my sake.
> You suffered both hunger and thirst for my sake.
> You taught, prayed, and fasted for my sake.
> All your holy works you performed for my sake.
> You suffered the most terrible pains and torments for my sake.
> Finally, you gave your most precious body and blood
>> to be shed on the cross for my sake.
Let your blood cleanse and wash away my sin.
> Let your righteousness hide and cover my unrighteousness.
Grant me, merciful Savior, that when death has shut the eyes of my body,
> the eyes of my soul may still behold and look upon you.
>> And when death has taken away the use of my tongue,
>>> may my heart still cry and say unto you,
>> "O Lord, into your hands I commend my soul;
>>> Lord Jesus receive my spirit!" Amen.

—John Foxe, *Book of Martyrs (The Life and Death of Thomas Cromwell)*

[4]

**Hymn:**

And are we yet alive,
   and see each other's face?
Glory and thanks to Jesus give
   for his almighty grace!

Preserved by power divine
   to full salvation here,
again in Jesus' praise we join,
   and in his sight appear.

## Praying in the Spirit of Christ

What troubles have we seen,
    what mighty conflicts past,
fightings without, and fears within,
    since we assembled last!

Yet out of all the Lord
    hath brought us by his love;
and still he doth his help afford,
    and hides our life above.

—*UMH* 553:1-4

# 5

## Genuine Peace

**Scripture:**

The peace of God that exceeds all understanding will keep your hearts and minds safe in Christ Jesus.

—Philippians 4:7

**Prayer:**

We dare to believe, O God, that true peace is possible in this life.
> We know that we must first "cast our anchor" in heaven,
>> because true peace cannot be found in the things of this world.
>> Earthly things are full of change; there is no security in them whatsoever.
> We know that genuine peace only comes from loving you.
>> If our lives are rooted in you, and we continuously practice your presence,
>>> then we will never be shaken or overwhelmed by what comes our way.

We know that the only thing that brings light to our world is the sun,
> and every cloud dims and hides it from our eyes.
> But the Light of lights shines with radiance into every pit,
>> and your glorious presence makes every circumstance a heaven
>>> for those who have eyes to see.
> What walls can keep out your infinite Spirit, for it fills all things?
> What darkness can there be where you shine supreme?
> What sorrow where you comfort?
> What sea can separate you from us?
> You alone are a thousand companions.
> You alone are a world of friends.

We dare to believe, O God, that if we have experienced this genuine peace,
> then our hearts are full of love.
> So we pour out our deepest desires,
>> our greatest fears into the heart of our invisible Friend,
>>> who loves us all the more as we ask more,
>>>> as we even complain more.
> So we lift up our prayer to the high throne of heaven!
>> No hour is unseasonable, no person too base,
>>> no words too simple, no request too great.

We dare to believe, O God that we can speak personally and confidently to you;
> and you hear us, answer us, and comfort us.
>> We place ourselves fully before you,
>>> and you freely offer yourself to us.
>> In you, O blessed Lord, we find our peace. Amen.

> —Joseph Hall, *Heaven Upon Earth; or, Of True Peace of Mind* [7]

**Hymn:**

Thou hidden source of calm repose,
    thou all-sufficient love divine,
my help and refuge from my foes,
    secure I am if thou art mine;
and lo! from sin and grief and shame
    I hide me, Jesus, in thy name.

Thy mighty name salvation is,
    and keeps my happy soul above;
comfort it brings, and power and peace,
    and joy and everlasting love;
to me with thy dear name are given
    pardon and holiness and heaven.

*—UMH* 153:1–2

# 6

## *Faith Working through Love*

**Scripture:**

Faith working through love does matter.

—Galatians 5:6

**Prayer:**
You have taught us, O God, that saving faith works through love.
> A pure heart, a good conscience, steadfast faith,
>> and true Christian love go hand in hand.
>
> If our faith is sound, we will feel a holy flame of most dear
>> and special love towards you in our hearts.
>
> When we possess a living faith, we love you for your love and goodness to us.
>> We love you because you loved us first.
>
> When we consider the happy and holy work of our new creation
>> and the mighty power of your sanctifying Spirit,
>>> we realize how you have pulled us from the edge of the precipice
>>> and snatched us as brands out of the fire to make us stars in heaven.
>>
>> This is such a marvelous mercy!

You have taught us, O God, to love you for your beauty and holiness,
> for all that incomprehensible majesty, purity, and glory,
>> which you infinitely and eternally possess.
> Help us, therefore, to love nothing in the world but for your sake.
> Help us, therefore, to love our friends, not for pleasure, profit, or reputation,
>> but because they have your image shining in them.
> Help us, therefore, not to love our health because it makes our lives easy and free,
>> but because it brings vigor to our bodies and liberty to our minds
>>> so we can serve you more cheerfully.
> Help us, therefore, not to love honors, knowledge, greatness, and prestige,
>> but to love others and engage in even more and greater good works,
>>> do more good unto all people, and glorify you.

You have taught us, O God, that if your love is planted deep in our hearts,
> it will spread to all people who also bear your image—
>> to all true Christians, because they are fellow members of Christ's body
>>> and co-heirs with us of the same kingdom.
> May the light we see in others truly reside in our own souls. Amen.

—Robert Bolton, *Treatise on Self-Examination* [9]

## Hymn:

Let us plead for faith alone,
> faith which by our works is shown;

God it is who justifies,
> only faith the grace applies.

## Praying in the Spirit of Christ

Active faith that lives within,
    conquers hell and death and sin,
Hallows whom it first made whole,
    forms the Savior in the soul.

Let us for this faith contend,
    sure salvation is the end;
heaven already is begun,
    everlasting life is won.

Only let us persevere
    till we see our Lord appear,
never from the Rock remove
    saved by faith which works by love.

*—UMH 385*

# 7

## *The Great Commandment*

**Scripture:**

He responded, "You must love the Lord your God with all your heart, with all your being, with all your strength, and with all your mind, and love your neighbor as yourself."

—Luke 10:27

**Prayer:**

Your Word commands me to love you, O God, with all my heart and with all my soul.
    It requires the whole stream of my affections, desires, and intentions—
        my whole being—to run to you.
    There is good reason for you to make such demands of me,
        because you have freely given me all that I am and all that I have.
        If you have given to me so fully, and I give only a part of myself in return,
            there is no mutuality in love.

## Praying in the Spirit of Christ

So what does it mean to love you
> with all my heart, all my being, all my strength, and all my mind?
> It means that I must devote every part of who I am to your service:
>> my mind to think of you and to meditate on your glorious works;
>> my memory to remember Christ, his benefits, and his commands;
>> my will to act out my love every day in imitation of Christ.

Your Word commands me to love you, O God, with all my heart and with all my soul.
> So plant this love in my heart—the greatest gift of your beloved Son.
> Through Christ you have done so much for me out of your abundant love;
>> you have fed me and clothed me;
>> you have given me every good thing out of your abundant joy;
> You love me Lord, and as fire sparks fire, so love sparks love.
> Just pondering your great love kindles a reciprocal love towards you in my heart.
>> You are worthy of my love.
>> You ask for nothing but my love in return.
>> You have planted love in my heart.
>> You call me your own.

Your Word commands me to love you, O God, with all my heart and with all my soul.
> So I offer you my whole heart freely.
>> I deeply desire to love you because you are
>>> the greatest lover of my soul. Amen.

—John Preston, *The Breast-Plate of Faith and Love (Part 2)* [9]

**Hymn:**

Thou, O Christ, art all I want,
    more than all in thee I find;
raise the fallen, cheer the faint,
    heal the sick, and lead the blind.

Just and holy is thy name,
    I am all unrighteousness;
false and full of sin I am;
    thou art full of truth and grace.

Plenteous grace with thee is found,
    grace to cover all my sin;
let the healing streams abound,
    make and keep me pure within.

Thou of life the fountain art,
    freely let me take of thee;
spring thou up within my heart;
    rise to all eternity.

*—UMH* 479:3-4

# 8

## *The Incarnation*

**Scripture:**

The Word became flesh and made his home among us. We have seen his glory, glory like that of a father's only son, full of grace and truth.

—John 1:14

**Prayer:**

You put on our human nature, O God, when your Son came to earth.
    In Jesus you experienced our infirmities, weakness, and miseries.
    Because your Son came, your great gifts may now abound in our lives;
        When you graft us into Christ through baptism,
            you enable us to participate in his dignity and his glory.
        You unite us intimately with the Second Person of the Trinity.
        How can we even comprehend this stupendous exaltation of
            our nature,
            that you should take us into the unity of your very Being?
Whatever Christ accomplished in our nature, O God, you did it.
    Since our very being is one with Christ
        —and all that he did on our behalf was done by you—

>   our union with Christ is inseparably fixed.
>     We are your sons and daughters
>       because he was the Son of Man, God in our flesh.
>   You unite us to yourself—the miracle is too wondrous:
>     the union of your nature with ours binds your divinity to our humanity;
>     this union of grace secures our communion with Christ;
>     the union of glory secures eternal life in him—in you.
>   You became human that we might be one with you.
> All we can do is stand in awe, O God, in the face of this great mystery:
>   Eternity entered time and space;
>   Blessedness itself became a curse;
>   He who was rich beyond all measure became poor for our sakes;
>   He who delighted in eternal companionship with you
>     relinquished those beams of glory for a time
>     that he might reconcile the whole world to you!
>   You came to us in the flesh—to think of this alone swallows up our thoughts.
>   All the articles of our faith yield to this one grand thing—
>     you came to us in the flesh. Amen.
>
>                                —Richard Sibbes, *God Manifest in the Flesh* [10]

**Hymn:**

Christ, by highest heaven adored;
Christ, the everlasting Lord;
late in time behold him come,
offspring of a virgin's womb.

Veiled in flesh the Godhead see;
hail th'incarnate Deity,
pleased with us in flesh to dwell,
Jesus, our Emmanuel.

## Praying in the Spirit of Christ

Hail the heaven-born Prince of Peace!
Hail the Sun of Righteousness!
Light and life to all he brings,
risen with healing in his wings.

Mild he lays his glory by,
born that we no more may die,
born to raise us from the earth,
born to give us second birth.

*—UMH* 240:2–3

# 9

## The Intercession of Christ

**Scripture:**

Who is going to convict them? It is Christ Jesus who died, even more, who was raised, and who also is at God's right side. It is Christ Jesus who also pleads our case for us.

—Romans 8:34

**Prayer:**

You sit at God's right hand as a judge and king, interceding Christ,
    having all power in heaven and earth;
    but you also sit enthroned on high in order to intercede for us.
    Your mighty acts on our behalf include your compassionate care
        and your continuous pleading on our behalf.
            If you are interceding for us, who is to condemn?
You are our High Priest, pleading Christ.
    Outside the holy of holies you have already sacrificed yourself once
        for all—
            you offered yourself willingly as a sacrifice unto death on the
                cross.

But you also ascended into heaven where you reign forever—
> in the holy of holies you now pray for us.

Not only have you provided the means by which our sins are forgiven,
> you serve as our advocate at the points of our deepest need.
>> The blood which you offered with tears and strong cries
>> on the cross
>>> you continue to offer up virtually with prayers in the
>>> heavens. On earth the sacrifice of your life was
>>> your primary act;
>> in heaven, your primary work is that of carrying us
>> perpetually
>>> into the presence of God.

Your intercession culminates your priesthood, most blessed Jesus.
> Like the great High Priest, none but you can approach the holy
> of holies.
> When you died on the cross, you brought your earthly mission
> to its climax;
>> in heaven you bring that mission to completion.

How can we ever find the words to thank you, redeeming Christ?
> You are always for us, always on our side, always interceding on our
> behalf! Amen.

—Thomas Goodwin, *The Triumphs of Faith from Christ's Intercession* [11]

**Hymn:**

Hail the day that sees him rise
to his throne above the skies!
Christ, awhile to mortals given,
reascends his native heaven.

There the glorious triumph waits:
lift your heads, eternal gates!
Christ hath conquered death and sin,
take the King of glory in.

See! the heaven its Lord receives,
yet he loves the earth he leaves;
though returning to his throne,
still he calls the world his own.

See! he lifts his hands above:
See! he shows the prints of love.
Hark! his gracious lips bestow
blessings on his church below.

*—UMH* 312

# 10

## *A Spirit of Power*

**Scripture:**

You will receive power when the Holy Spirit has come upon you, and you will be my witnesses in Jerusalem, in all Judea and Samaria, and to the end of the earth.

—Acts 1:8

**Prayer:**

You are a spirit of power in us, O God, by being in us a spirit of truth.
> Your Spirit not only leads us into all truth—into the Word—which is the only truth,
>> but also leads the truth into us until we become inseparably one with you.
>> Not only is your Spirit a spirit of truth to us, she is a spirit of power.

You are a spirit of power in us, O God, by being in us a spirit of wisdom.
> Make us wise with your wisdom—wise upon earth, wise to salvation.
>> We know there is no wisdom apart from your Spirit;
>>> all other wisdom is mere foolishness to you.

> But the wisdom of your Spirit is heavenly wisdom.
>> It is our genuine and indubitable strength.
> Your wisdom is far more precious than the strength of the world,
>> for it can do greater things than earthly strength.
> Not only is your Spirit a spirit of wisdom to us, she is a spirit of power.

You are a spirit of power in us, O God, by being in us a spirit of faith.
> Faith is your work, and no less power works faith in us
>> than that which raised Christ from the dead.
>>> So carry us out of ourselves to Christ.
>> Through the power of faith enable us both to do and to endure
>>> the same things that Christ himself did and endured.
>>> Like Paul, help us to say, "I can endure all these things through the power of the One who gives me strength."
>> Your power is not finite but infinite, not a particular but a universal power.
>> Through the power of faith enable us not only to do some things,
>>> but to do all things through Christ who strengthens us.
>> Not only is your Spirit a spirit of faith to us, she is a spirit of power. Amen.
> —William Dell, *Christ's Spirit, Christians' Strength* [12]

**Hymn:**

Spirit of faith, come down,
   reveal the things of God,
and make to us the Godhead known,
   and witness with the blood.
'Tis thine the blood to apply
   and give us eyes to see,
who did for every sinner die
   hath surely died for me.

## Praying in the Spirit of Christ

Inspire the living faith
 (which whosoe'er receive,
the witness in themselves they have
 and consciously believe),
the faith that conquers all,
 and doth the mountain move,
and saves whoe'er on Jesus call,
 and perfects them in love.

*—UMH* 332:1, 4

# 11

## *Growing in Love*

**Scripture:**

We have known and have believed the love that God has for us. God is love, and those who remain in love remain in God and God remains in them.

—1 John 4:16

**Prayer:**

Plant a passionate disposition of love towards you, O God, in my heart.
    Make this love the chief good and ultimate goal of my life.
    Set this love as the measure by which I judge everything else.
    I want this loving end to determine the nature of all the means I use.
        Establish a principle within me not to practice any means
            that are inconsistent with the ultimate goal or end of love.
    I do many things in my life that do not answer to this grand end.
        How many purposes, desires, words, and actions have I embraced
            that are inconsistent with what I claim as the goal of my life?

> I live for myself and not for you.
> I invest in things that seduce me away from you as my chief end.
> Plant a continuous disposition of love towards you, O God, in my heart.
> It is not enough for me to resign my heart to you, O God,
> as I did when I first experienced your love;
> rather, I need to beg often that you reclaim me
> from this yearning after those things that pull me
> away from love as my true and noble end.
> Unless you maintain this love in me, and sustain it constantly,
> what would become of me?
> Plant a transforming disposition of love towards you, O God, in my heart.
> My unwillingness to obey—and the tedium I find in obedience—
> reveals the great imperfection in my love.
> You must reshape my love. You must increase it.
> You must excite it. You must keep it active.
> I must exercise it often.
> I want Paul's prayer to be my own,
> that your love might become even more and more rich in my life.
> I want the fire of my love to be blown up into a flame.
> I want your love to take up residence in my heart.
> Sanctify me fully as I seek nothing other than greater love in my heart and life. Amen
>
> —Thomas Manton, *Sermons (2 Thessalonians 3:5)* [12]

**Hymn:**

Jesus, thine all victorious love
   shed in my heart abroad;
then shall my feet no longer rove,
   rooted and fixed in God.

O that in me the sacred fire
   might now begin to glow;
burn up the dross of base desire
   and make the mountains flow!

O that it now from heaven might fall
   and all my sins consume!
Come, Holy Ghost, for thee I call,
   Spirit of burning, come!

Refining fire, go through my heart,
   illuminate my soul;
scatter thy life through every part
   and sanctify the whole.

*—UMH 422*

# 12

## *God Is Gracious*

**Scripture:**

The Lord is good to everyone and everything; God's compassion extends, to all his handiwork!

—Psalm 145:9

**Prayer:**

You are such an incomprehensible fusion of righteousness and grace, O God.
    When I consider your power and your transcendent glory, great Jehovah,
        fear lays hold of my soul and I want to flee from your presence;
            I need to be reminded of your goodness and love:
    You are compassionate and merciful, very patient,
        full of great loyalty and faithfulness,
            demonstrating your steadfast love to a thousand generations.

Jesus has revealed your gracious and personal nature to me.
> He revealed your infinite goodness and mercy in the flesh;
>> Your name is also Emmanuel—God with us.
> In Christ I see you as a human being—my brother.

Oh! that name, Jesus!
> Your name brings healing for every wound,
>> serenity for every distraction,
>>> comfort for every sorrow.

Through the power of the Spirit,
> remind me of your coming to us in the flesh;
>> your tender dealing with all sorts of sinners;
>>> your care of your own.

Oh my soul, believe;
> never cry out, "my sins, my sins!"

Out of the abundance of your love, O gracious Lord, pardon all my sins.

Help me to understand and experience the power of the gospel—
> the sum of the whole gospel—Jesus came to save me! Amen.

—Isaac Ambrose, *Looking Unto Jesus* [16]

**Hymn:**

How can we sinners know
   our sins on earth forgiven?
How can my gracious Savior show
   my name inscribed in heaven?

What we have felt and seen,
   with confidence we tell,
and publish to the ends of earth
   the signs infallible.

## Praying in the Spirit of Christ

We who in Christ believe
    that he for us hath died,
we all his unknown peace receive
    and feel his blood applied.

We by his Spirit prove
    and know the things of God,
the things which freely of his love
    he hath on us bestowed.

*—UMH* 372:1–4

# 13

## *The Presence of God*

**Scripture:**

God isn't far away from any of us. In God we live, move, and exist. As some of your own poets said, "We are his offspring."

—Acts 17:28

**Prayer:**

Your presence fills all things, close and loving God.
    In you we live, and move, and have our being.
        You are fully present in every place,
            not bound with cords, except the bonds of love.
    You hold the great expanse of the heavens in your hand.
        You spin the earth with your foot.
        You guide all the creatures with your eye.
        You refresh all things with your influence.
        You fill the hearts of your people with your Holy Spirit.
        You reign in the hearts of your servants; we find your kingdom there.

## Praying in the Spirit of Christ

You are in us, O God, and we are in you.
    You made us for good works
        so grant us grace to be your hands and feet in this world.
        Open our eyes to see the needs of our brothers and sisters;
        open our ears to hear the cry of the needy and desolate;
            open our hands to provide drink for the thirsty,
        food for the hungry, and clothes for the naked.
You make every place, person, and situation sacred, O God, by virtue of your presence.
    Help us to be ready, therefore, at every moment to do good.
        Since you are present in every creature,
            we must be cruel toward none—abusive toward none.
    Help us to walk as in your presence, O God,
        to turn to you in every need,
        to seek your strength in every moment of doubt,
        to open our hearts to you,
        to weep before you on account of our sins,
        to revere you as Lord,
        to obey you as our loving Parent. Amen.
            —Jeremy Taylor, *Rules and Exercises of Holy Living* [16]

**Hymn:**

Maker, in whom we live,
    in whom we are and move,
the glory, power, and praise receive
    for thy creating love.
Let all the angel throng
    give thanks to God on high,
while earth repeats the joyful song
    and echoes to the sky.

Eternal, Triune God,
    let all the hosts above,
let all on earth below record
    and dwell upon thy love.
When heaven and earth are fled
    before thy glorious face,
sing all the saints thy love hath made
    thine everlasting praise.

—*UMH* 88:1, 4

# 14

## *The Light of Christ*

**Scripture:**

This is the message that we have heard from him and announce to you:
"God is light and there is no darkness in him at all."

—1 John 1:5

**Prayer:**

O Dayspring from on high, O Splendor of eternity,
    O spotless Mirror of the divine majesty,
      you are the true light that shines on all people!
        Come, and enlighten the darkness of my blindness and
          ignorance,
            and let my affection so feel your divine radiance,
              that my heart may burn and melt like wax before you.
    O help me to see and hear you, my heavenly Master.
    Make me to behold light in your light by perfect love flaming up in
        my heart.

May I have a continual sensation of you and of the divine essence in
  you,
    that I may be renewed according to your image, conformed to
      your likeness, and made in my soul like a mirror image of
      your holiness.
You are the true Light that enlightens everyone coming into this world.
  Come, and drive away the darkness from the face of the abyss of my
    mind,
      that I may see you and know you.
  O Light! which no other light can see;
    Brightness! which no other brightness can behold.
  O Light! without which all light is darkness,
    come and swallow me up in the abyss of your love.
      May I see myself in you everywhere I go—you in me and all
      things in you.
Open my eyes, O divine Teacher.
  O most high God! invariable and unchangeable, subsisting by yourself,
    creator of all good, from whom all good things flow.
  O uncreated Wisdom, who radiates our minds with your brilliant
    rays,
  take all distractions of my mind away,
    raise me up to desire you alone,
    enable me to experience unity with the Father,
      who draws and attracts souls, and is the fountain of all
      life.
    Bind me to you with the sweet cords of your love
      that I may be more enkindled by your blaze and united to
      you in love.
  Lead me into the innermost chambers of your love
    that I may behold your immutable light upon my mind. Amen.

—Francis Rouse, *Academia Celestis* [16]

## Praying in the Spirit of Christ

**Hymn:**

Christ, whose glory fills the skies,
    Christ, the true, the only Light,
Sun of Righteousness, arise,
    triumph o'er the shades of night;
Dayspring from on high, be near;
Day-star, in my heart appear.

Visit then this soul of mine;
    pierce the gloom of sin and grief;
Fill me, Radiancy divine,
    scatter all my unbelief;
more and more thyself display,
shining to the perfect day.

*—UMH* 173:1, 3

# 15

## *God's Commandments*

**Scripture:**

This is the love of God: we keep God's commandments.

—1 John 5:3

**Prayer:**

Christ did not come into the world, O God, to fill our heads with speculations,
    to kindle a fire of wrangling among us,
        or to inflame our spirits against one another with angry and peevish debates, while in the meantime our hearts remain all ice towards you
            and have no spark of true heavenly fire to melt them.
Christ did not come, O God, to possess our brains only with some cold opinions
    that send down nothing but a freezing and numbing influence on our hearts.

May our hearts beat with the truest pulse towards heaven;
> Give us honest and good hearts,
>> ready to comply with Christ's commandments.

Fill our hearts with a passionate desire to obey the law of love,
> so that our minds might be renewed according to your image
>> in righteousness and true holiness.

Help us to understand that the smallest amount of heartfelt affection towards you
> is more satisfying to our souls than all the speculations in the world.

Help us to understand that nothing but the life of Christ deeply rooted in our hearts
> provides sustenance for our souls.

Help us to root and center our lives in you,
> rather than merely contemplating and gazing upon you.

Help us to anchor ourselves in you,
> even though we are not able to comprehend fully
>> the Alpha and Omega of our faith.

Help us to understand that the only way to really know you
> is to obey Christ's law of love. Amen.

—Ralph Cudworth, *The Life of Christ* [17]

**Hymn:**

Come, divine Interpreter,
  bring me eyes thy book to read,
ears the mystic words to hear,
  words which did from thee proceed,
words that endless bliss impart,
kept in an obedient heart.

All who read, or hear, are blessed,
    if thy plain commands we do;
of thy kingdom here possessed,
    thee we shall in glory view
when thou comest on earth to abide,
reign triumphant at thy side.

*—UMH* 594

# 16

## *Love Divine*

**Scripture:**

Now faith, hope, and love remain—these three things—and the greatest of these is love.

—1 Corinthians 13:7

**Prayer:**

My soul yearns for union with you, O God, because of the nature of your love.
    Your love elicits reciprocal love;
        it unites my mind and heart with you—its proper object.
    Your love for me arises out of the overflowing of your own immense goodness.
        You are love, and herein is love, not that I loved you,
            but that you loved me, and sent your only begotten Son.

You bind me to yourself through love;
> I follow you as nearly as I can, thirsting and panting after you.

Your love engenders within me, O God, a deep desire and intense endeavor to be like you.
> My trust in you transforms my life—my faith becomes effective in love.
>
> Only your indwelling love can change my soul into the likeness of Christ.
>> To love you is the only way and means to be like you, for you are love.

Because I have experienced your unconditional love,
> I joyfully ascribe all glory and honor to you.
>
> Whenever I remember your holiness,
>> I break forth in praise.
>
> My praise is nothing other than an outward expression
>> of the inward contemplation of your perfect love.
>
> My responsive love rejoices in all those things
>> through which your name is praised.

Your divine love, O God, is a love of deep friendship.
> I revel in the intimate fellowship that we share.
>> You dwell in me, and I dwell in you.
>
> Through the power of your Spirit
>> keep our bond of friendship strong and my heart open;
>>> come to me continually and make your home in me.
>
> You share your love with me so freely
>> and promise to live in my heart forever. Amen.

—John Owen, *Christologia (Part 2)* [18]

## Praying in the Spirit of Christ

**Hymn:**

Love divine, all loves excelling,
    joy of heaven, to earth come down;
fix in us thy humble dwelling;
    all thy faithful mercies crown!
Jesus, thou art all compassion,
    pure, unbounded love thou art;
visit us with thy salvation;
    enter every trembling heart.

Breathe, O breathe thy loving Spirit
    into every troubled breast!
Let us all in thee inherit;
    let us find that second rest.
Take away our bent to sinning;
    Alpha and Omega be;
end of faith, as its beginning,
    set our hearts at liberty.

*—UMH* 384:1–2

# 17

## *The Desire of the Heart*

**Scripture:**

Enjoy the Lord, and he will give what your heart asks.

—Psalm 37:4

**Prayer:**

Two fundamental principles, O God, shape my deepest longings:
    The fact that my relationship with you is the purpose of my life
        and the fact that this relationship is my joy.
    My prayer is that these thoughts will greet me first thing every
        morning—
        that my mind will be settled and habituated in my relationship
            with you.
I desire to love you and Christ Jesus my Redeemer,
    with all my mind, all my heart, all my soul, and all my strength.
I desire to lose myself in meditation every time I think of you,
    and Christ as the author, fountain, and substance of all my happiness;
    all-sufficient, only sufficient for my soul, and all comfort and good.

## Praying in the Spirit of Christ

I desire to die daily. I do not mean that I daily wish for death,
> but that I may be prepared for it at any time.

I desire to improve every relationship of my life
> that glory may be given to Christ by my being
>> a child to one, a brother to another, a neighbor to a third, a friend.

I desire to redeem all time from vain thoughts and meaningless chatter.

I desire to guard time for those things that nurture my soul
> and lead to true godliness, particularly daily prayer and time spent with God.

I desire to interact with others in such a way that all are strengthened,
> encouraged, and secured by the bond of love.

I desire to view the Sacrament of the Lord's Supper
> as the bread that came down from heaven,
>> the water of life, spiritual wine and milk, and nourishment for my soul.

I desire to account those my best friends that most help me in my Christian walk
> and to esteem those who watch over me in love—
> whose faithful admonitions are the best expressions of friendship.

To Jesus, with the Father, and the Holy Ghost,
> be all glory, and love, and faith, and obedience, rendered forever! Amen.

—Herbert Palmer, *Memorials of Godliness and Christianity* [20]

**Hymn:**

I want a principle within
   of watchful, godly fear,
a sensibility of sin,
   a pain to feel it near.
I want the first approach to feel
   of pride or wrong desire,
to catch the wandering of my will,
   and quench the kindling fire.

Almighty God of truth and love,
   to me thy power impart;
the mountain from my soul remove,
   the hardness from my heart.
O may the least omission pain
   my reawakened soul,
and drive me to that blood again,
   which makes the wounded whole.

*—UMH* 410:1, 3

# 18

## *Give Thanks*

**Scripture:**

Whatever you do, whether in speech or action, do it all in the name of the Lord Jesus and give thanks to God the Father through him.

—Colossians 3:17

**Prayer:**

We give you thanks, O God, for your unfailing goodness.
    We model our lives after the practice of Jesus,
        who, in the meal he shared with his disciples,
            gave thanks to you, took bread, blessed it, broke it,
            and gave it to those he loved;
        who, on the ship with a company of his hungry followers,
            took bread and gave thanks to you in the presence of them all.
    We model our lives after the practice of the earliest followers of Jesus,
        who shared their food with gladness and generous hearts.

*Give Thanks*

Can we receive any good gift from you, O God, without thanksgiving?
> For whenever we express the genuine thankfulness of our hearts,
>> we do service acceptable to you and comfort our own souls.
>
> You have given us so many reminders of our need
>> to be thankful for all that you have done.
>
> Grant us grace to express our gratitude not only in outward words and ways,
>> but with a true and inward disposition of gratitude for all your good gifts.
>
> Grant us grace to bring all our requests to you in our prayers and petitions,
>> along with giving thanks.
>
> Grant us grace to summon every ounce of our energy to bless you
>> for all we have received from your hand.
>
> Whenever we offer up our thanks sincerely and faithfully,
>> whenever we proclaim that it is right and a joyful thing
>>> to give you thanks and praise,
>>>> our hearts cry out with a cheerful yet humble confidence,
>>>> "Amen, so be it."
>
> Crown our "Amen," O generous God,
>> by blessing us—your children—even as we have blessed you.
>> Amen.

—Robert Sanderson, *Sermons* [20]


**Hymn:**

Come and let us sweetly join,
Christ to praise in hymns divine;
give we all with one accord
glory to our common Lord.

## Praying in the Spirit of Christ

Hands and hearts and voices raise,
sing as in the ancient days;
antedate the joys above,
celebrate the feast of love.

Jesus, dear expected Guest,
thou art bidden to the feast;
for thyself our hearts prepare;
come, and sit, and banquet there.

Sanctify us, Lord, and bless,
breathe thy Spirit, give thy peace;
thou thyself within us move,
make our feast a feast of love.

*—UMH 699*

# 19

## *Pray Continually*

**Scripture:**

Pray continually.

— 1 Thessalonians 5:17

**Prayer:**

I worship you, great God of love; my true worship consists in acknowledging who you are.
> I worship you with my soul and my body.
>> I love to pray to you in worship because it is just like speaking to you.
>>> My prayer reflects all those things I need to do in your presence.

I confess my sins, acknowledging them with honesty before you.
> I am sinful by nature, so I confess who I am: broken and needy.
> I confess those specific actions and attitudes that separate me from you and others.

## Praying in the Spirit of Christ

In the community of faith I confess with my brothers and sisters that all of us
> have failed to be your obedient children.

In the quiet of my heart I confess how often I fall short as your child—
> the loving person you have created me to be.

I am truly sorry, O God, and acknowledge my great unworthiness.
> You know me better than I know myself, so change me from the inside out.

I offer my supplications, begging you for the desires of my heart.
> I ask for your Spirit to enable me to turn away from my sins and walk in obedience.
> I plead for all the virtues—faith, hope, and love,
>> and especially for all those qualities I lack.
>
> I desire those things I need to be healthy and whole.

I intercede for others, praying for all who need your love and care.
> I pray for all those in affliction or distress,
>> particularly those persons I hold dear in my heart.
>
> I pray for those who have wounded me,
>> for those who have abused me and lied about me,
>>> for those who have stolen my dreams to serve their own purposes.
>
> I ask that you bless them with all good things as you have blessed me.

I thank you, praising you for all your great mercies to me and others.
> I thank you for revealing your true self to me in Jesus,
>> for sending the Spirit, and for all those means you have used to bring me home.
>
> I praise you for your patience and long-suffering,
>> waiting for my repentance, and not cutting me off in my sins.

> I praise you for all the blessings of life;
>> for health, friends, food, clothing,
>>> and for those interventions by which your gracious providence
>>>> kept me from falling and delivered me from danger.
> With a thankful heart I remember the many ways in which
>> you have brought goodness, truth, and beauty to my life.
>>> Amen.
>
> *—The Whole Duty of Man (Part IV)* [21]

**Hymn:**

> Pray without ceasing, pray,
> (your Captain gives the word)
> His summon cheerfully obey
>> and call upon the Lord;
>> to God your every want
>> in instant prayer display,
> pray always, pray and never faint,
>> pray, without ceasing pray.
>> From strength to strength go on,
>> wrestle and fight and pray,
> tread all the powers of darkness down
>> and win the well-fought day.
>> Still let the Spirit cry
>> in all his soldiers, "Come!"
> till Christ the Lord descends from high
>> and takes the conquerors home.
>
> *—UMH* 513:3-4

# 20

## *The Altar of the Heart*

**Scripture:**

A continuous fire must be kept burning on the altar; it must not go out.

—Leviticus 6:13

**Prayer:**

Lord, I have turned my back on your friendship so many times.
    I have transferred my love from you to other things,
        Only your mercy can pardon my wayward spirit and restore my soul;
        only you can enable me love to you as I ought—my deepest desire.
Lord, I am so grateful for your mediation—for the way you offer me mercy and peace.
    You entered into this world, suffered, and died to heal my disease.
    You purchased my reconciliation because of your abiding commitment to me.
        I am set free to love as I ought because of your great work of redemption.

Lord, I owe all my love and gratitude to you.
> I want to live more fully by faith in you because you are my hope of salvation.
> I want to put my entire self into your hands because all good things come from you.

Lord, rekindle the fire of divine love on the altar of my heart.
> Extinguish my misdirected love and redirect it to its proper end.
>> I need to offer you my whole heart and nothing else.
>> I must permit no rival love in my heart.
>> I know that when I offer my heart fully and entirely to you,
>>> you enter it, and dwell in it, and fill it with divine light and joy.
> I desire nothing but this, to recover your love in my heart.

Lord, fill my heart then—my soul—with light and joy.
> Overwhelm me with your grace and restore my soul.
>> Instruct. Allure. Persuade. Excite.
>> Work within me both to do and to will.
>>> If I truly desire to place your love on the altar of my heart,
>>>> I know that you will be faithful to grant what I ask.

Lord, God of Light and Love, deluge me with the blessings of heaven.
> To the all-good, all-wise, and all-mighty Lord our God,
>> Father, Son, and Holy Spirit, be praise and glory forever. Amen.

—James Garden, *Comparative Religion* [22]

**Hymn:**

O Thou who camest from above,
   the pure celestial fire to impart,
kindle a flame of sacred love
   upon the mean altar of my heart.

## Praying in the Spirit of Christ

There let it for thy glory burn
  with inextinguishable blaze,
and trembling to its source return,
  in humble prayer and fervent praise.

Jesus, confirm my heart's desire
  to work and speak and think for thee;
still let me guard the holy fire,
  and still stir up thy gift in me.

Ready for all thy perfect will,
  my acts of faith and love repeat,
till death thy endless mercies seal,
  and make my sacrifice complete.

—*UMH* 501

# 21

## *The Face of God*

**Scripture:**

God said that light should shine out of the darkness. He is the same one who shone in our hearts to give us the light of the knowledge of God's glory in the face of Jesus Christ.

—2 Corinthians 4:6

**Prayer:**

If we seek you, O God, we will surely find you.
    You do not put obstacles in our way when we search for you.
    You surround us with your light when we seek your face.
    You convict us of our misery when we try to live without you,
        and offer us the infinite mercy of Christ when we return.
    You unite our spirits with Christ;
        you replenish our souls with humility, joy, confidence, and love.
    You offer us peace in Christ alone; we find no delight, no joy, but in your love.
Two things, O God, obstruct our reconciliation with you: self-love and low desire.

## Praying in the Spirit of Christ

Help us to acknowledge our own brokenness and our need of Christ—our Mediator.
> We need you so desperately, for only you create a path to hope.

Help us to experience the love of Jesus in the face of hopelessness.
> We need you continually, for only you can give us eyes to behold your glory.

Help us to open our hearts to the spiritual healing you offer us through your Spirit.
> We cannot know you, O God, without acknowledging our own brokenness;
>> we cannot know our own brokenness without acknowledging you;
>
> we cannot know you without acknowledging our need for Jesus;
>> we cannot know Jesus until we experience the ways in which
>>> he heals our wounds and repairs our broken lives.

You have revealed your true self, O God, in the face of Jesus Christ.
> You are the very center and supreme object of our lives.
>> You are the source of all our hopes and aspirations.
>>> You are the way to understanding and light.
>>>> You are the One who shows us the true meaning of life.

When we see you, O God, in the face of Jesus Christ,
> we see also into the depths of our own souls.
>> We know ourselves fully in you.
>>> We find all our happiness and all our virtue,
>>>> our life and light, our hope and assurance in you.
>>> Amen.

—Blaise Pascal, *Pensées* [23]

**Hymn:**

Thou hidden love of God, whose height,
    whose depth unfathomed no one knows,
I see from far thy beauteous light,
    and inly sigh for thy repose;
my heart is pained, nor can it be
    at rest, till it finds rest in thee.

Is there a thing beneath the sun
    that strives with thee my heart to share?
Ah, tear it thence and reign alone,
    the Lord of every motion there;
then shall my heart from earth be free,
    when it hath found repose in thee.

*—UMH* 414:1, 3

# 22

## *Humility*

**Scripture:**

He has told you, human one, what is good and what the Lord requires from you: to do justice, embrace faithful love, and walk humbly with your God.

—Micah 6:8

**Prayer:**

Humility, O God, disposes me to repentance,
    making me sensible of the infinite gap between who you are and who I am.
    I confess my moral imperfections, my sins and transgressions;
        I acknowledge that only you are righteous.
    When I am proud, murmuring and complaining arise in my spirit.
        Self-conceit makes me misconstrue all your actions towards me.

# Humility

When I am humble, I am so sensible of the myriad ways
    in which I have missed the mark.
    You appear most just, even gentle, in the ways you woo me home.
        I see how I have been unreasonable, unrighteous, and disingenuous.
            I realize how myopic my vision is at times
                and how unfathomable your ways.
                Your riches, wisdom, and knowledge are so deep!
                    They are as mysterious as your judgments,
                        and they are as hard to track as your paths.
I acknowledge how holy, wise, and good you are,
    how you always have my best interest at heart.
Humility, O God, disposes me to patience,
    making me more receptive to your grace.
        The more I seek to be empty and poor in spirit,
            the more earnestly I desire spiritual things.
Humility, O God, disposes me to gratitude,
    making me fit to receive more from your hand;
        I am so grateful and gladly give you all glory and praise.
Humility, O God, disposes me to faith and love,
    making faith in Christ and love for you well up within me. Amen.

                —John Worthington, *Self-Resignation* [24]

**Hymn:**

'Tis mercy all that thou hast brought
    my mind to seek its peace in thee;
yet while I seek, but find thee not,
    no peace my wandering soul shall see.
O when shall all my wanderings end,
    and all my steps to theeward tend?

## Praying in the Spirit of Christ

Each moment draw from earth away
    my heart that lowly waits thy call;
speak to my inmost soul and say,
    "I am thy love, thy God, thy all!"
To feel thy power, to hear thy voice,
    to taste thy love, be all my choice.

—*UMH* 414:2, 5

# 23

## This Holy Mystery

**Scripture:**

I received a tradition from the Lord, which I also handed on to you: on the night on which he was betrayed, the Lord Jesus took bread. After giving thanks, he broke it and said, "This is my body, which is for you; do this to remember me." He did the same thing with the cup, after they had eaten, saying, "This cup is the new covenant in my blood. Every time you drink it, do this to remember me."

—1 Corinthians 11:23–25

**Prayer:**

O holy Jesus, as I approach your holy table
    I repent of my sins sincerely, steadfastly desiring to lead a new life.
    Cultivate within my heart a lively trust in your mercy,
        a thankful remembrance of your death,
            a love of all people and a desire for true reconciliation.
    Foster within my heart a lively trust in your sacrifice on the cross
        for the sins of the whole world, and particularly for mine.

## Praying in the Spirit of Christ

O holy Jesus, when at the altar I see the bread broken and the wine poured,
> remind me of your suffering through those sacred and significant signs,
>> how your blessed body was scourged, wounded, and bruised
>>> and how your precious blood was shed for my sins.
> May this remembrance set all my powers at work to love you
>> and to celebrate your love in thus dying for me.

O holy Jesus, at your holy table dispose my heart to be your guest,
> that I may feel all the sweet influences of Love crucified,
>> strengthening and refreshing my soul,
>>> as my body and soul are by the bread and wine.
>>>> Offer new grace, new life, new love, new vigor,
>>> and new resolution through your immortal food.
> When I devoutly receive the outward elements,
>> may I also receive you through the bread and the wine.

O holy Jesus, you invite me to your heavenly feast.
> Give me grace to approach this holy mystery with a heart full of love for you.
>> Settle in my soul a lively faith in your mercy through Christ
>>> and a steady belief in all your love.
>> May I pant after you that I may admire and adore you;
>>> may I take heavenly delight in your gracious presence;
>>>> offer you my praise and thanksgiving
>>>>> and receive you into my heart.

O holy Jesus, the only gifts I have to offer you are myself and my love.
> So help me always to walk in love as you have loved me
>> and have given yourself for me;
>>> I offer my life as a well-pleasing sacrifice to you. Amen.

—Thomas Ken, *Exposition of the Catechism* [25]

**Hymn:**

O the depth of love divine,
    the unfathomable grace!
Who shall say how bread and wine
    God into us conveys!
How the bread his flesh imparts,
    how the wine transmits his blood,
fills his faithful people's hearts
    with all the life of God!

Sure and real is the grace,
    the manner be unknown;
only meet us in thy ways
    and perfect us in one.
Let us taste the heavenly powers,
    Lord, we ask for nothing more.
Thine to bless, 'tis only ours
    to wonder and adore.

*—UMH* 627:1, 4

# 24

## *Communion with God*

**Scripture:**

I pray they will be one, Father, just as you are in me and I am in you. I pray that they also will be in us, so that the world will believe that you sent me.

—John 17:21

**Prayer:**

Creative God, you have made nothing gloomy or dismal.
    No slaves are born into your great house of this world.
    You have made all things out of yourself;
        You cannot make anything evil or desolate.
        Everything that you have made is good, beloved, blessed.
    You were free to make the world, or not.
        Everything is the product of your almighty love and goodness.

## Communion with God

Creative God, our happiness consists in living into what you have created us to be.
> If we act in ways that are aligned with your design, we experience true happiness.
> The nearer we come to you, the greater our happiness.
>> Happiness grows on the basis of our deepening communion with you.
>>> and there can be no communion without likeness.
>>> The sun shines on a stone wall as well as on a person,
>>>> but a stone wall has no communion with the sun
>>>>> because it has no eyes to see the light.
>>> Neither can a stone wall receive the benefits of your heat.
>>> A log of wood lies in the water as well as the fish,
>>>> but it has no communion with the water,
>>>>> nor receives any of its advantages as the fish does.

Creative God, our lives in you are not meant to be heavy or plodding, but active and vital.
> We yearn for the life and vigor that come from you, for you are Life itself.
> You are the very center of our being
>> and offer to us the fullness of your energy and vitality.
>>> Help us to embrace you in the fullness of your being.

Creative God, make us one in a communion of genuine mutuality and reciprocity.
> We cannot participate in your life unless we surrender ourselves to you.
> We have nothing to offer to you other than our whole selves.
>> Help us to offer ourselves back to you
>>> as well as to take you into our souls.
>> Help us to shake off that lazy and drowsy spirit
>>> which has so numbed us in this stupid age of the world;
>> Help us to work out our salvation with care and diligence!
>>> Amen.

—Samuel Shaw, *Communion with God* [25]

Praying in the Spirit of Christ

**Hymn:**

Blest be the dear uniting love
    that will not let us part;
our bodies may far off remove,
    we still are one in heart.

Joined in one spirit to our Head,
    where he appoints we go,
and still in Jesus' footsteps tread,
    and do his work below.

O may we ever walk in him,
    and nothing know beside,
nothing desire, nothing esteem,
    but Jesus crucified!

We all are one who him receive,
    and each with each agree,
in him the One, the Truth, we live;
    blest point of unity!

*—UMH* 566:1–4

# 25

## *God's Providential Care*

**Scripture:**

I know the plans I have in mind for you, declares the Lord; they are plans for peace, not disaster, to give you a future filled with hope.

—Jeremiah 29:11

**Prayer:**

You have taken such good care of us, O God, through all our days.
    You have been with us when we have gone through the water
        and when we have passed through the fire.
    How miraculously you have appeared in our rescue.
        Your providential care has always been for our benefit.
        You have assisted us, comforted us, guarded and guided us,
            and moved us with the Spirit more times than we can count.
        You have done so much more for us than we could ever have imagined.

## Praying in the Spirit of Christ

How wonderful, O God, are all your works.
> In wisdom you made all things.
>> The earth is full of your riches!
> We are bound to magnify your goodness!
>> How excellent, how vast, how all-encompassing it is!
>>> It is not confined to a day, nor restrained to a place,
>>>> nor limited to an hour!
>> From our cradles to this very moment you have preserved us
>>> and we have tasted daily how gracious you are.
>> You carry us on your wings as the eagle does her young.

Through all the various stages of our lives, O God,
> we have witnessed so many miracles of providence!
> Truly, Lord! Your mercy and patience
>> ought to be our song in the house of our pilgrimage!
> Of this, and this alone, we have reason to boast,
>> to talk about and meditate on day and night.
> We exist because of your providence and goodness.
>> It supports, feeds, maintains, and preserves us
>>> through every event of life.

O let your mercy melt our hearts, O God!
> O let mercy prevail with us to give up ourselves fully to you!
> Let mercy and goodness constrain us to love you!
> O let your love be of such force in our souls
>> that we are unable to resist its motions.
> By the strength of your love may we hope, believe, endure,
>> and love and obey you to the end of our days,
>>> through Jesus Christ our Lord. Amen.

—Anthony Horneck, *Happy Ascetic* [28]

**Hymn:**

O that the world might taste and see
    the riches of his grace!
The arms of love that compass me
    would all the world embrace.

Thee I shall constantly proclaim,
    though earth and hell oppose;
bold to confess thy glorious name
    before a world of foes.

His only righteousness I show,
    his saving truth proclaim;
'tis all my business here below
    to cry, "Behold the Lamb!"

Happy, if with my latest breath
    I may but gasp his name,
preach him to all and cry in death,
    "Behold, behold the Lamb!"

*—UMH* 193:3–6

# 26

*Follow the Spirit*

**Scripture:**

If we live by the Spirit, let's follow the Spirit.

—Galatians 5:25

**Prayer:**

Following your Spirit, O God, means
 to live under the guidance of the Spirit,
  to live in the power of the Spirit,
   and to live a spiritual life.
 If we follow the Spirit, then we are your sons and daughters.
Graciously enable us to live under the guidance of the Spirit.
 Enlighten us and open our minds so that we may understand the Scriptures,
  for the Bible provides directions for the way.
 Take us by the hand, as it were, and lead us:
  like a shepherd tends the flock
   and gathers lambs in his arms and lifts them onto his lap.

Graciously enable us to live in the power of the Spirit.
> Carry us forward on our holy pilgrimage,
>> fulfilling all the expectations this entails,
>>> under the influence and assistance of the Holy Spirit.
> Without Christ—without the assistance of his Spirit—we cannot do anything,
>> Help us to follow those directions and intimations of your will
>>> that you give us out of the Word,
>>>> and those impulses of the Spirit upon our hearts.

Graciously enable us to live spiritual lives.
> Help us to keep our focus on you and your way
>> and on those spiritual practices in which we meet and serve you.
> Help us to contemplate, and admire, and adore
>> your infinite beauty and incomprehensible perfections,
>>> your unspeakable love, and grace, and goodness towards us.
> Help us to explore the mysteries of Christ
>> and study the riches and mystery of the gospel.
> Help us to rejoice in our worship of you, O God.
>> May our prayer and spiritual reading be pleasant to us
>>> because we meet you—our beloved Friend—in them.
>> You meet us in your Word; you meet us in our prayers and fasting.
> By beholding your face in these ways you change us as we follow the Spirit,
>> from glory to glory into your image and likeness. Amen.

—Richard Alleine, *Vindication of Godliness* [30]

Praying in the Spirit of Christ

**Hymn:**

Come, Holy Ghost, our hearts inspire,
    let us thine influence prove;
source of the old prophetic fire,
    fountain of life and love.

Come, Holy Ghost (for moved by thee
    the prophets wrote and spoke),
unlock the truth, thyself the key,
    unseal the sacred book.

Expand thy wings, celestial Dove,
    brood o'er our nature's night;
on our disordered spirits move,
    and let there now be light.

God, through the Spirit we shall know
    if thou within us shine,
and sound, with all thy saints below,
    the depths of love divine.

—*UMH* 603

# 27

## The Gospel Feast

**Scripture:**

Every day, they met together in the temple and ate in their homes. They shared food with gladness and simplicity.

—Acts 2:46

**Prayer:**

Your Gospel Feast is so important to me, O Lord,
    You gave us this sacred meal as a means of gathering your church together.
    At the table I experience what it means to be part of your body.
        I share some little pieces of the consecrated bread
            dipped in the sacramental cup,
                and I am joined with you and my brothers and sisters
                      in the bond of love.
    I love to contemplate the idea that, every Lord's Day, all around the world
        my brothers and sisters gather together around the same meal.

## Praying in the Spirit of Christ

This meal has fed your family since the very beginning, O Lord.
    The church has lived a constant rhythm that moves from Word to Table.
        Help me to fix the eye of my mind on you—the crucified Savior.
        The more often I commune with you at the table,
            the stronger and healthier I feel,
                the more able to encounter the difficulties of life.
        You nourish your family every day through this meal;
            the gospel becomes more real in my life as you feed me here.
You instituted this Holy Supper in a private house, O Lord.
    The earliest apostles celebrated this meal in the homes of believers;
        The rich and the poor often feasted together at the same table.
        They testified and confirmed their mutual love and kindness at these meals. They viewed this sacrament, not only as a seal of peace with God,
            but also as a sign and a pledge of communion
            and fellowship one with another.
I love to sing hymns and psalms as I receive my food
    with a glad and generous heart.
I feel connected in this way with all who have come before me.
    Here I encounter you—the living Word—present in spirit and in truth.
At your table, O Lord, I receive nourishment for my soul;
    it is here that you bind us together in the bond of love. Amen.

        —William Cave, *Primitive Christianity (Chapter 11)* [31]

**Hymn:**

Come, sinners, to the gospel feast;
let every soul be Jesus' guest.
Ye need not one be left behind,
for God hath bid all humankind.

Sent by my Lord, on you I call;
the invitation is to all.
Come, all the world! Come, sinner, thou!
All things in Christ are ready now.

Come, all ye souls by sin oppressed,
ye restless wanderers after rest;
ye poor, and maimed, and halt, and blind,
in Christ a hearty welcome find.

This is the time, no more delay!
This is the Lord's accepted day.
Come thou, this moment, at his call,
and live for him who died for all.

*—UMH* 339:1–3, 5

# 28

## *The Sacred Meal*

**Scripture:**

Listen! I am standing at the door, knocking; if you hear my voice and open the door, I will come in to you and eat with you, and you with me.

—Revelation 3:20

**Prayer:**

You shine upon me, O God, in the face of Jesus Christ.
    You call me to a paradise of delight.
    You invite me to a table where you reveal your beloved Son to me,
        the express image of your person,
            and all the fruits of holiness manifest in Christ's earthly life.
Awaken my spirit, O God, to reflect on all Christ's miraculous works of love,
    his holy and useful life, his bitter passion, his shameful death,
        his glorious resurrection and ascension,
            his power at your right hand on high,
    and all the benefits of his life, death, and resurrection
        offered freely to me.
Stir up every ounce of my energy to bless his holy name.

In your sacrament, O God, what a new world I see:
> You fill me with good hope, peace, and joy in the Holy Spirit.
>> O, what a glorious sight. It even overwhelms the angels who behold it on high!
>>> I want your new creation to characterize my life;
>>>> I want to be changed into the image of Christ,
>>>>> from glory to glory, by your loving Spirit!

I will come to you, O God, for I place my hope and comfort in your love.
I will come to you, O God, for I long to be changed more and more into your divine image
> and I am resolved to abide in you so that your Word shall abide in me.

I will come to you, O God, to renew my covenant with you
> by making a cheerful sacrifice of all that I am, and have, and can do,
>> to your service.

Let it be so, O God, according to your word.
> I ask for nothing other than the grace to abide in your love,
>> that I may grow and increase in wisdom and holiness.
> I ask for nothing but to be filled with all the fruits of the Spirit,
>> with love, joy, peace, patience, kindness, goodness,
>> faithfulness, gentleness, and self-control,
>>> and that they may abound in me
>>>> more and more to your praise and glory. Amen.

—Simon Patrick, *Christian Sacrifice (Fifth Meditation)* [32]

**Hymn:**

O Thou who this mysterious bread
   didst in Emmaus break,
return, herewith our souls to feed
   and to thy followers speak.

### Praying in the Spirit of Christ

Unseal the volume of thy grace,
    apply the gospel word;
open our eyes to see thy face,
    our hearts to know the Lord.

Of thee communing still, we mourn
    till thou the veil remove;
talk with us, and our hearts shall burn
    with flames of fervent love.

Enkindle now the heavenly zeal,
    and make thy mercy known,
and give our pardoned souls to feel
    that God and love are one.

*—UMH 613*

# 29

## *The Weight of Sin*

**Scripture:**

I most certainly don't want anyone to die! This is what the Lord God says.
  Change your ways, and live!

—Ezekiel 18:32

**Prayer:**

We reflect on our sin, O God, and want to turn away,
  but do not let us be content with just a cursory glance.
    Enable us to ponder our sins that your fire may burn within us.
      Our consciences have often told us that we are guilty.
      Enable us to ponder these things in our hearts!
Hear our cry, O God, "What have we done! How have we provoked you!"
  We remember our sins, with all their aggravations.
      We put our past sins in a present view, and own them all.
        How many days, or years, have we lived
          in some of these addictions and cycles of brokenness.

We weigh the accrued burden of our sin until our hearts are broken.
We pray with the Psalmist, "My wrongdoings are stacked higher than my head;
> they are a weight that's way too heavy for me."
We acknowledge our pride and carelessness,
> but put all into one great sum that it may humble our hearts.
We present ourselves before you, O God, in your glory and holiness,
> and upon our knees we bless your holy name
> by confessing to you all those sins that we can remember.
> Like Joshua we give glory to you; we want to tell you all we have done;
> we don't want to hide anything from you.
We confess all our low and unworthy thoughts of you,
> all our anger towards you, your laws, and people.
We confess what envy, what malice, what rancor, has festered in our hearts.
We confess all our sins and ask for you to do away with them and our hard hearts.
> We do not want to add sin to sin because of a formal, dull confession.
> If our hearts have become callused and hard,
> take away the heart of stone.
> We lay this all before your throne of grace.
> We lay ourselves before you and ask earnestly for you
> to shatter the rock that the waters of life may spring out.
> Amen.

—Lewis Stuckley, *A Gospel Glass* [33]

**Hymn:**

Sinners, turn: why will you die?
God, your Savior, asks you why.
God, who did your souls retrieve,
died himself, that you might live.
Will you let Him die in vain?
Crucify your Lord again?
Why, you ransomed sinners, why
will you slight his grace and die?

Turn, he cries, ye sinners turn;
by his life your God hath sworn;
he would have you turn and live,
he would all the world receive;
he hath brought to all the race
full salvation by his grace;
he hath not one soul passed by;
why will you resolve to die?

*—UMH* 346:1, 7

# 30

## *Arise, Shine*

**Scripture:**

Arise! Shine! Your light has come; the Lord's glory has shone upon you.

—Isaiah 60:1

**Prayer:**

Lord Jesus, you are our light and our salvation.
> We extoll your light and the glory of the gospel, for you are the image of God.
> You are the sun and the gospel is the sphere in which you give light to your people.
> You said that whoever follows you won't walk in darkness
>> but will have the light of life.
> With Simeon we declare that you are a light for revelation to the Gentiles,
>> and for glory to your people Israel.
> All the prophets and evangelists magnify your light and praise you forever.

Lord Jesus, you are the eternal Son of God:
> Co-eternal with God, you appeared in our world,
>> wrapped up in the darkness of human nature.
> You are the Dayspring from on high who has visited us,
>> to give light to those who are sitting in darkness.
> You are the sun of righteousness, full of purity and righteousness,
>> as the sun is of light, all luminous, without spot,
>>> subject to no eclipse, since your light is your own.
>>> Like the sun, your light is not diminished
>>>> when you impart it to others who behold it together;
>>> nor is your righteousness diminished when you confer it on us.

Lord Jesus, you invite us—sinners though we are—to come to you
> so that you might offer your grace freely to all.
>> The sun has a vivifying power.
>>> And so, you are the life that is the light for all people.
>> The sun drives away the sharp frosts and the heavy fogs of winter.
>>> And so, you banish all our fears, warm our hearts,
>>>> strengthen our faith, and cure all our spiritual sickness.
>> You come with healing in your wings.

Lord Jesus, all darkness flees away before you.
> Your light can never be taken away. Amen.

>> —Robert Leighton, *Sermons* (Isaiah 60:1) [35]


## Hymn:

Glory to God, and praise and love
   be ever, ever given,
by saints below and saints above,
   the church in earth and heaven.

### Praying in the Spirit of Christ

On this glad day the glorious Sun
    of Righteousness arose;
on my benighted soul he shone
    and filled it with repose.

O for a thousand tongues to sing
    my dear Redeemer's praise!
The glories of my God and King,
    the triumphs of his grace.

My gracious Master and my God,
    assist me to proclaim,
to spread through all the earth abroad
    the honors of thy name.

—*UMH* 57:1–2, 7–8

# 31

## Our Daily Labor

**Scripture:**

Whatever you are capable of doing, do with all your might because there's no work, thought, knowledge, or wisdom in the grave, which is where you are headed.

—Ecclesiastes 9:10

**Prayer:**

You have given us work, O God, to preserve and perfect our nature.
    It keeps us in good tune and temper,
        improving and advancing us toward our best state.
    The labor of our mind in attentive meditation and study
        makes it capable of thinking about those things that matter
            most.
    Work rouses our spirits, directing them into their proper channels.
    The simple work of our body keeps the organs sound and clean.
        If water runs, it remains clear, sweet, and fresh,
            but stagnation turns it into a rancid puddle.

## Praying in the Spirit of Christ

> Air fanned by the wind remains pure and wholesome,
>> but when shut up it grows thick and putrid.
> Metals that are used remain smooth and splendid,
>> but set them aside and rust begins to consume them.
> We know that the preservation and improvement of our spiritual lives
>> depends on our constant effort and work.

You designed us for work, O God, not intending for us to be idle.
> The fairest fruits and the richest rewards come from our labor.
> In fact, all good things are the fruits of our work,
>> ordered to sprout from it under the influence of your blessing.
>> All good things, indeed, are your gifts,
>>> freely dispensed by your hand.
>> But you do not give them absolutely without condition,
>>> nor miraculously apart from ordinary means.
>> That would deprive us of the sweet contentment
>>> which springs from enjoying the fruit of our labor.

Therefore, may we work, O God, while it is still day.
> Grant us happiness, eternal life in perfect rest, joy, and glory, as we work for you.
> Help us to work out our salvation with fear and trembling,
>> for climbing this holy mountain requires effort.
>>> Give us the strength we need to work for your glory.
>>> Amen.

—Isaac Barrow, *Sermons (Ecclesiastes 9:10)* [35]

**Hymn:**

Forth in thy Name, O Lord, I go,
  my daily labor to pursue;
thee, only thee, resolved to know
  in all I think or speak or do.

## Our Daily Labor

The task thy wisdom hath assigned,
    O let me cheerfully fulfill;
in all my works thy presence find,
    and prove thy good and perfect will.

Thee may I set at my right hand,
    whose eyes mine inmost substance see,
and labor on at thy command,
    and offer all my works to thee.

For thee delightfully employ
    whate'er thy bounteous grace hath given;
and run my course with even joy,
    and closely walk with thee to heaven.

*—UMH 438*

# 32

## *Our Refuge and Strength*

**Scripture:**

God is our refuge and strength, a help always near in times of great trouble.

—Psalm 46:1

**Prayer:**

You have placed me within the covenant of grace, O God, that I might have abundant life.
> In Christ you have provided everything that I need to feel secure.
>> Lord Jesus, you are a compassionate, tender-hearted Mediator.
>> Lord Jesus, you have power and authority over everything in my life.
>> Lord Jesus, you want to help me, as your disciple, in every possible way.
>> Lord Jesus, you are a tender brother, a careful shepherd,
>>> an empathetic high priest, a loving husband, a sympathetic leader,
>> a life-giving root, an all-sufficient king.

Lord Jesus, you can calm my mind and comfort my heart
> when I am drooping and discouraged—when my soul
>> faints.

Through the Spirit you have provided everything that I need to grow.
> Holy Spirit, you have helped me to wrestle through and
>> overcome
>>> all difficulties and discouragements that were in my way.
> Holy Spirit, you have offered me life when I was faint-hearted,
>> heart-broken, and discouraged.
> Holy Spirit, you have interceded for me when I had no words of
>> my own
>>> to offer in supplication at the throne of grace.
> Holy Spirit, you have revived my heart when I was ready to give
>> up.
> Holy Spirit, you have always listened to me and heard my cry,
>> lifting up my head in hope and putting a song in my
>>> heart.

As a loving Parent, you have provided everything I need to be who I am.
> Love Divine, I cast all my discouragements, entanglements,
>> and difficulties—as burdens too heavy—on you.
> Love Divine, I leave them in your care because you are the only
>> One
>>> who can handle them, resolve them, remove them from
>>>> my life.
> Love Divine, carry me through.
>> Help me to look to Jesus, the Author and Finisher of my
>>> faith,
>>>> as the source of my courage in life.
>> Help me to rely on the Spirit, the Power and Energy of love,
>>> as the source of my strength in the race of life.
>>>> Amen.

—John Brown, *Christ the Way, the Truth, and the Life* [36]

## Praying in the Spirit of Christ

**Hymn:**

O Love, how cheering is thy ray!
    All pain before thy presence flies!
Care, anguish, sorrow, melt away
    where'er thy healing beams arise.
O Jesu, nothing may I see,
nothing hear, feel, or think, but thee!

In suffering be thy love my peace,
    in weakness be thy love my power;
and when the storms of life shall cease,
    Jesu, in that important hour,
in death as life be thou my guide,
and save me, who for me hast died.

*—UMH* 183:3-4

# 33

## *The Saints' Rest*

**Scripture:**

Therefore, since the promise that we can enter into rest is still open, let's be careful so that none of you will appear to miss it.

—Hebrews 4:1

**Prayer:**

Holy God, those who have completed their pilgrimage in faith inspire me daily.
    I want to be able to claim a crown of righteousness like theirs.
    They possess the security of an eternity with you that is perfect.
        I long for that perfect blessedness that comes from knowing you fully.
Holy God, I know that my true happiness consists in obtaining
    the prize of that upward call in Jesus Christ.
        Help me to keep fixed on that as the principal goal of my life
            and not any subordinate or lesser end.

I do not want to pursue this goal—this upward call—as a mercenary.
My rest is not something I should expect as if it were wages for work done.
Your command to "do this and live" is far more than a covenant of works.
>Your law of grace tells me to believe in Christ, to seek him,
>>to obey him sincerely as my Lord and King, to forsake all,
>>>to suffer all things, and to overcome,
>>>>and by so doing, or in so doing, I shall live.
Help me to live abundantly like this by putting my trust in Christ.
Holy God, my glorification of you and your salvation of me
>are not two different purposes or ends, but one.
>I bring you the greatest glory when I live as your child, fully alive!
>>Help me to aim at your glory, therefore,
>>>not as something separate in any way from my salvation,
>>>>but in and through it.
Like St. Paul, I want to be able to say, "I have fought the good fight,
>finished the race, and kept the faith."
Holy God, help me to be devoted fully to this one end.
>Create a spirit within me that desires nothing but to glorify you,
>>and if it is your good pleasure, grant me an everlasting rest
>>>because I belong to Christ. Amen.

—Richard Baxter, *The Saints' Everlasting Rest* [37]

**Hymn:**

Come, let us join our friends above
who have obtained the prize,
and on the eagle wings of love
to joys celestial rise.
Let saints on earth unite to sing
with those to glory gone,
for all the servants of our King
in earth and heaven are one.

Our spirits too shall quickly join,
like theirs with glory crowned,
and shout to see our Captain's sign,
to hear this trumpet sound.
O that we now might grasp our Guide!
O that the word were given!
Come, Lord of Hosts, the waves divide,
and land us all in heaven.

—*UMH* 709:1, 4

# 34

## *A Clear Conscience*

**Scripture:**

I have committed myself to maintaining a clear conscience before God
  and with all people.

—Acts 24:16

**Prayer:**

My heart and my spirit, O God, are bound together in my conscience.
  You witness through my conscience through a kind of silent reasoning of the mind.
  My conscience judges things to be good and true
    on the basis of a deep inward affection of the heart.
  My conscience approves the right and the good with delight.
    But those things which are evil it disapproves with sorrow.
You have placed this conscience within me, O God, for a purpose.
  It examines all my actions, both toward you and other people.
  It determines the health of our relationship,
    whether my service is inward and spiritual or only outward and formal.

It surveys all my duties—all those spiritual actions of the heart,
> revealing to me whether I pray in faith, listen with attention,
> receive you in your Holy Meal—in short—
> whether I maintain an intimate connection with you or not.

The great object of my conscience is a right relationship with you and with others.

Open my heart and mind, O God, to the sunshine of Scripture
> so that nothing will ever be able to quench the flame of my conscience.
>> Convict me of sin and move me to action.
>> Reveal my indifference toward actions I know to be wrong.
>> Uncover the evil I disguise in the good that I do.
>> Bind my soul to your truth so that I may maintain a clear conscience.

Help me listen to my conscience, O God, and permit it to direct
> both my attitudes and my actions,
>> for it will always align my life with your loving will. Amen.

—Matthew Poole, *Sermons (Acts 24:16)* [38]

## Hymn:

O come and dwell in me,
   Spirit of power within,
and bring the glorious liberty
   from sorrow, fear, and sin.

Hasten the joyful day
   which shall my sins consume,
when old things shall be done away,
   and all things new become.

I want the witness, Lord,
   that all I do is right,
according to thy mind and word,
   well-pleasing in thy sight.

## Praying in the Spirit of Christ

I ask no higher state;
    indulge me but in this,
and soon or later then translate
    to thine eternal bliss.

—*UMH* 388

# 35

## *Doers of the Word*

**Scripture:**

You must be doers of the word and not only hearers who mislead themselves.

—James 1:22

**Prayer:**

You command us to act as well as to rest, O God, to be doers of the word and not hearers only.
> You nourish us both inwardly and outwardly in our spirits through our actions.
>> You have created us in such a way that our love deepens through
>>> practices and actions in which you promise to meet us.

## Praying in the Spirit of Christ

Engagement in practices of the spirit, O God, quiets our hearts.
> Save us from the desire to abandon the means you have provided!
> You promised the Israelites the land of Canaan,
>> but they did not sit idle in anticipation of what you would do for them.
>> When they took possession of Canaan they cultivated grain;
>>> they did not presume that you would simply supply manna.
> Jesus never taught us to run to miracles
>> when there are things we can do for ourselves.

But having affirmed this, O God, we know you provide the harvest of grace.
> That great gift comes from our use of the means you have ordained.
> Without you, nothing we do ever satisfies or suffices fully;
>> You consummate all our actions and fill them with meaning.

Help us, O God, to avail ourselves of every opportunity to draw close to you.
> Save us from the error of thinking that, since we are saved by grace,
>> we have no part to play in our relationship with you.
> Inspire us to be active participants in our unfolding life together.
> Help us to practice the means of grace—to be doers of your word.
> Help us to embrace the practices of the spirit
>> as our constant companions in the journey of faith.
> Help us to acknowledge our dependence on you for everything,
>> so that we never mistake the means— our actions—as ends in themselves.
> Help us to practice the means faithfully,
>> and then rest in your presence and your promise of abundant life. Amen.

—Edward Crane, *A Prospect of Divine Providence* [38]

**Hymn:**

Come, let us use the grace divine,
    and all with one accord,
in a perpetual covenant join
    ourselves to Christ the Lord;
Give up ourselves, thru Jesus' power,
    his name to glorify;
and promise, in this sacred hour,
    for God to live and die.

The covenant we this moment make
    be ever kept in mind;
we will no more our God forsake,
    or cast these words behind.
We never will throw off the fear
    of God who hears our vow;
and if thou art well pleased to hear,
    come down and meet us now.

*—UMH* 606:1–2

# 36

## *Patience in Suffering*

**Scripture:**

Come to me, all you who are struggling hard and carrying heavy loads,
    and I will give you rest.

—Matthew 11:28

**Prayer:**

By holding fast to you, O God, we will gain our lives.
    We lose our souls by impatience;
        but when we submit to you without grumbling,
            we rest in peace and we know we are yours.
    We confess that we are often impatient,
        wanting what we do not have and not wanting what we have.
    We are enslaved by our impatient souls! What weakness! What error!
By holding fast to you, O God, we will experience peace in our lives.
    Inward peace does not come simply with the alleviation of suffering
        in our lives;
        rather, we experience peace when we relinquish everything into
            your hands.

## Patience in Suffering

Your merciful hand executes what we would never have had the courage to do;
> Your mercy enables us to endure with patience.

You offer us the medicine sometimes which we do not have the strength to choose.

By holding fast to you, O God, we embrace the cross.
> Since we belong to Christ, help us to imitate his suffering—even the cross.
>> The more we fear our crosses, the more reasons we conceive
>>> as to why we should not have to endure them.
>> When we are called to carry heavy burdens, help us to learn in patience.
>>> Help us never to forget that you are committed to our cure.
>>> Help us to draw a source of love, comfort, and trust in you
>>>> from our very afflictions
>> Remind us of the timeless truths from scripture:
>> Blessed are those who mourn.
>> Those who plant with tears reap the harvest with joyful shouts.
>> Those who go out, crying and carrying their seed,
>>> come home with joyful shouts, carrying bales of grain.
> When we feel like we are fastened to the cross with Christ,
>> may your grace sustain us there.
> O suffering and adorable Jesus!
>> Help us to unite with you in your sacrifice.
>> Help us to think less of our own suffering
>>> and more about the happiness of suffering with you.
>> Help us to trust you so deeply that we do not fear the cross. Amen.

—François Fénelon, *Letters* [38]

## Praying in the Spirit of Christ

**Hymn:**

Jesus, lover of my soul,
    let me to Thy bosom fly,
while the nearer waters roll,
    while the tempest still is high.
Hide me, O my Savior, hide,
    till the storm of life is past;
safe into the haven guide;
 O receive my soul at last.

Other refuge have I none,
    hangs my helpless soul on thee;
leave, ah! leave me not alone,
    still support and comfort me.
All my trust on thee is stayed,
    all my help from thee I bring;
Cover my defenseless head
    with the shadow of thy wing.

*—UMH* 479:1–2

# 37

## *Seek the Lord*

**Scripture:**

Seek the Lord when he can still be found; call him while he is yet near.

—Isaiah 55:6

**Prayer:**

You know best what I need, O God, and all that you do is for my good.
    If I could only accept how much you love me
        I would be ready to receive whatever comes my way in life.
        I would simply be pleased by the fact that everything comes
           from you.
    I view so many of my afflictions in a wrong light.
        But when I see them as a part of your providential design
           —when I know you are shaping me through all I
               endure—
                my suffering loses its bitterness
                    and even becomes a matter of consolation.

## Praying in the Spirit of Christ

Grant me the grace to pour all my energies, therefore, into knowing you,
    for the more I know you, the deeper my longing to know you more;
        the deeper my knowledge of you, the greater my love for you;
            and the greater my love for you, the more easily I embrace my path.
    Free me from the desire to love you merely for what I can get from you.
        I know this will never bring us close to one another;
            rather, instill within me a genuine trust in you
                because this creates an intimate connection in one simple act.
Grant me the grace to seek you often by faith—
    to chase everything else out of my heart
        except the desire to love and please you.
    Only you can work in my soul the great change to which I aspire—
        the inner peace and tranquility you have promised to us all.
        I pray for this more than anything else
            and desire it for every one of your children. Amen.
    —Brother Lawrence, *Practicing the Presence of God (Letters)* [38]

**Hymn:**

By thy reconciling love
every stumbling block remove;
each to each unite, endear;
come, and spread thy banner here.

Make us of one heart and mind,
gentle, courteous, and kind,
lowly, meek, in thought and word,
altogether like our Lord.

Let us for each other care,
each the other's burdens bear;
to thy church the pattern give,
show how true believers live.

Free from anger and from pride,
let us thus in God abide;
all the depths of love express,
all the heights of holiness.

—UMH 562:2–5

# 38

## *Practicing the Presence*

**Scripture:**

I am with you now, I will protect you everywhere you go, and I will bring you back to this land. I will not leave you until I have done everything that I have promised you.

—Genesis 28:15

**Prayer:**

We long to practice your presence, O God, and request your grace
    to renounce everything not leading to you;
        to enjoy a continual conversation with you, in freedom and simplicity;
        to recognize your intimate presence within us at every moment;
        to beg your assistance in knowing your will and following it completely,
            which we plainly see you require of us;
        to offer every action to you before we do it and thank you for its
            completion;
        to engage in continual conversation with you;
        to praise, adore, and love you incessantly for your infinite goodness
            and perfection;

to seek your mercy with a perfect confidence,
> without being discouraged on account of our defects,

to give us light in our doubts when we have no other design but to please you;

to sanctify our actions when they are completed only for your sake;

to do the work you have given us to do without any view to pleasing others,
> but purely (and as far as possible) for your love's sake;

to pray unceasingly, praising you and blessing you with all our might,
> passing our lives in continual joy;

to put our whole trust in you, and make a total surrender of ourselves to you,
> secure in the knowledge that you will never let us down;

to love you and others more perfectly in our lives,
> knowing we are totally dependent upon your grace at every moment. Amen.

—Brother Lawrence, *Practicing the Presence of God (Conversations)* [38]

## Hymn:

Christ, from whom all blessings flow,
perfecting the saints below,
hear us, who thy nature share,
who thy mystic body are.

Join us, in one spirit join,
let us still receive of thine;
still for more on thee we call,
thou who fillest all in all.

Move and actuate and guide,
Diverse gifts to each divide;
placed according to thy will,
let us all our work fulfill;

## Praying in the Spirit of Christ

Never from thy service move,
needful to each other prove;
use the grace on each bestowed,
tempered by the art of God.

—*UMH* 550:1-4

# 39

## *Heart Religion*

**Scripture:**

Create a clean heart for me, God; put a new, faithful spirit deep inside me!
—Psalm 51:10

**Prayer:**

It would be useless to seek you, O God,
> if the distance between us were insurmountable; but you are so very close to us.

We make the prayer of St. Augustine our own:
> I sought you, O my God, in heaven, in earth, and in the creatures,
>> but I did not find you there.
>
> I sought you far off, but you were very near.
> As soon as I sought you in my heart, I found you there.

## Praying in the Spirit of Christ

> We pray to you, O God, with faith, confidence, and love, and always from the heart.
> > We implore you to send your Spirit to teach us how to pray.
> > > We are only children and we don't know what to say.
> > > > Send your Spirit to help us in our weakness,
> > > > > for she will plead our case with unexpressed groans.
>
> You have taken us into your heart, O God, as a loving Parent.
> > We ask for you to fill our hearts with gratitude.
> > You delight in loving us, in excusing our weaknesses, and in forgiving us.
> > We ask for you to fill our hearts with peace,
> > > to rest in your loving arms without any other care than to do your will.
> > 
> > We know that whenever, by the Spirit of adoption, we cry only this word, Abba,
> > > you hear and accept our heartfelt plea.
>
> Grant us a sense of your divine presence, O God, in our hearts.
> > Reveal your will to us in the daily dispensations of your providential care
> > > and in our heart-felt desire to follow it faithfully,
> > > > we cheerfully accept all that comes our way. Amen.
>
> —Susanna Wesley, *A Mother's Advice to Her Daughter* [38]

**Hymn:**

O for a heart to praise my God,
   a heart from sin set free,
a heart that always feels thy blood
   so freely shed for me.

A heart resigned, submissive, meek,
    my great Redeemer's throne,
where only Christ is heard to speak,
    where Jesus reigns alone.

A humble, lowly, contrite heart,
    believing, true, and clean,
which neither life nor death can part
    from Christ who dwells within.

A heart in every thought renewed,
    and full of love divine,
perfect and right and pure and good,
    a copy, Lord, of thine.

—*UMH* 417:1–4

# 40

## *Genuine Spirituality*

**Scripture:**

Accept each other with love, and make an effort to preserve the unity of the Spirit with the peace that ties you together.

—Ephesians 4:2b–3

**Prayer:**

Shape a genuine spirituality within us, O God, so we can put everything into your hands.
> We seek to enter your presence always in faith.
> We seek to love you with all our heart and spirit.
> We seek hearts characterized by lowliness—humble, gentle, and patient.
> We seek a quiet and serene evenness of heart and mind in times of turmoil.
> We seek a tranquility in which no news frightens us,
>> no success enflames our pride,
>>> and no tribulation shatters our confidence in you.
>
> Fill us with holy awe—a wonderful peace, constancy, and serenity of spirit.

Shape a genuine spirituality within us, O God, so we have a true sense of
>ourselves.
>>We confess our weaknesses and imperfections.
>>We confess our inordinate pride and trust in our own good works.
>>We confess our hesitancy to endure the ridicule of others for your
>>>sake
>>>>and to suffer the refinement and purification that this entails.
>>We confess our reluctance to die to self and our desire
>>>to grow in holiness by the means of sweetness and consolation.
>>Fill us with holy passion—a conformity to the way of the cross.

Shape a genuine spirituality within us, O God, so we can embrace your
>wisdom.
>>We desire to be filled with sweetness, governed by courage,
>>>and enlightened by the Spirit of divine wisdom.
>>We desire the indwelling Spirit through whom simplicity and liberty
>>>flourish.
>>We desire for our hearts of be enflamed with a deep affection for your
>>>way.
>>We desire to be filled with all the fullness of your love.
>>We desire to celebrate the gifts your wise Spirit has bestowed upon us.
>>Fill us with holy wisdom—a desire to be bound to one another
>>>by one Lord, one faith, one baptism, and one God and Father
>>>>of all,
>>>>>for you are over all, and through all, and in all.
>>>>>>—Miguel de Molinos, *The Spiritual Guide (Part 2)* [38]

**Hymn:**

All praise to our redeeming Lord,
>who joins us by his grace,

and bids us, each to each restored,
>together seek his face.

## Praying in the Spirit of Christ

He bids us build each other up;
    and, gathered into one,
to our high calling's glorious hope
    we hand in hand go on.

E'en now we think and speak the same,
    and cordially agree,
concentered all, through Jesus' name,
    in perfect harmony.

We all partake the joy of one;
    the common peace we feel,
a peace to sensual minds unknown,
    a joy unspeakable.

*—UMH* 554:1–2, 4–5

# 41

*Liberty in Christ*

**Scripture:**

If the Son makes you free, you really will be free.

—John 8:36

**Prayer:**

I yearn to be free, O God, but I need a clear sense of what freedom really means.
>    Some people conceive Christian liberty as deliverance from Mosaic Law.
>>        But this simply infers freedom from a yoke;
>>>            there must be something more than this.
>    Others view freedom as exemption from human laws.
>>        But the folly and wickedness of these opinions sufficiently confute them. Disobedience and anarchy are as flat a contradiction
>>>            to the peace that God offers as hedonism and opulence are to purity.

## Praying in the Spirit of Christ

I know from your Word, O God, that two things are essential to genuine freedom:
> a clear vision of what is good and a power to act in conformity to it.
>> Darkness and impotence constitute my slavery;
>>> my freedom consists of your light and strength.
>> Sin stands resolutely as the great obstacle to my liberty.
>> Sin obscures the light and renders impotent my capacity to do good.

But your grace in Christ brings victory, O God, to me and all your children.
> My impotence and inability to do those things you command bind me.
>> I desire more than anything else to do good, but I cannot do it.
> I seek the ability not only to will, but to do good, so that I might obey your holy, just, and good commandments.

I know that if I seek to be free, O God, you must make me so.
> Rescue me from servitude to sin and set me free to live as your obedient child.
> If I know the truth, certainly you can set me free through it.
> I give you thanks and praise, because you give me the victory
>> through Jesus Christ my Lord. Amen.

—Richard Lucas, *An Inquiry after Happiness (Part 3)* [41]

**Hymn:**

And can it be that I should gain
   an interest in the Savior's blood!
Died he for me? who caused his pain!
   For me? who him to death pursued?
Amazing love! how can it be
   that Thou, my God, shouldst die for me?

He left His Father's throne above
    (so free, so infinite his grace!),
emptied himself of all but love,
    and bled for Adam's helpless race.
'Tis mercy all, immense and free,
    for O my God, it found out me.

Long my imprisoned spirit lay,
    fast bound in sin and nature's night;
thine eye diffused a quickening ray;
    I woke, the dungeon flamed with light;
my chains fell off, my heart was free,
    I rose, went forth, and followed Thee.

—*UMH* 363:1, 3–4

# 42

*Resurrection Joy*

**Scripture:**

Death has been swallowed up by a victory. Where is your victory, Death? Where is your sting, Death?

—1 Corinthians 15:55

**Prayer:**

O God, you have glorified our victorious Savior with a visible, triumphant resurrection from the dead and ascension into heaven where he sits at your right hand, the world's supreme Governor and final Judge: grant that his triumphs and glories may ever shine in our eyes,

to make us more clearly view life through his sufferings, and more courageously endue our own; being assured by his example, that if we endeavor to live and die like him for the advancement of your love in ourselves and others, you will raise again our dead bodies too,

and conforming them to his glorious body, call us above the clouds, and give us possession

## Resurrection Joy

of your everlasting kingdom; through the same Lord Jesus Christ your Son, who, with you and the Holy Spirit, live and reign, one God, world without end. Amen.

> Arise, my soul, to you these joys belong; arise, and advance yourself on high.
>
> Leave here below all earthly thoughts, and fly away with the wings of the spirit.
>
> Fly to that glorious land of promise, and gladly salute those heavenly regions.
>
> Hail, happy paradise of pure delights; you beauteous garden of never fading flowers!
>
> Hail, blessed society of beatified spirits, who perpetually contemplate God!
>
> Hail, and forever may your glories grow, till they rise so high, they can grow no more.
>
> Hail you, who, in your cheerful songs remember us
>> who dwell below in this vale of tears.
>
> We hope one day to come up to you and be placed to sing in your holy choirs.
>
> O what a fire of love will it kindle in our hearts,
>> when we shall see those shining mysteries!
>
> Under veils you hide those glorious mysteries,
>> too high and spiritual for flesh and blood.
>
> O what excessive joy will that love produce;
>> a love so violently desiring, and so fully satisfied!
>
> When our capacities shall be stretched to the utmost
>> and your love fill and overflow them!
>
> Without losing what we are, we shall become in a great measure even what he is!
>
> We shall take part in all his joys, and share in the glories of all his heaven.
>
> There, O my soul, we shall rest from our labors,
>> which are but the way to all that happiness.

## Praying in the Spirit of Christ

There we shall rest forever in God, in the arms and bosom of our dearest Lord.

O heaven! the eternal source of all these joys,
    and infinitely more, and infinitely greater.

As the heart pants after the water brooks, so let my soul thirst after you.

When shall I be satisfied with that torrent,
    which springs forever from your glorious throne?

Come and here begin to dwell in my heart; and fit me for the life I shall lead hereafter.

Come and prepare my soul for you;
    and then, when it pleases you, take it to yourself. Amen.

—*Devotions for Great Festivals* [42]

**Hymn:**

Christ the Lord is risen today
earth and heaven in chorus say.
Raise your joys and triumphs high,
sing, ye heavens, and earth reply.

Lives again our glorious King.
Where, O death, is now thy sting?
Once he died our souls to save;
Where's thy victory, boasting grave?

Soar we now where Christ has led,
following our exalted Head;
made like him, like him we rise,
ours the cross, the grave, the skies!

King of glory, soul of bliss,
everlasting life is this:
Thee to know, thy power to prove,
thus to sing, and thus to love.

*—UMH* 302:1, 3-4, 6

# 43

## *The Glorious King*

**Scripture:**

Mighty gates: lift up your heads ancient doors: rise up high! So the glorious king can enter!

—Psalm 24:7

**Prayer:**

You have bound yourself to me, O Christ, by your promise.
> I feel so secure in you because your word is settled in heaven.
> Whatever you have promised, I can be absolutely sure about,
>> as if I had the thing in my own hand.
> However dark my circumstances may seem to be, I will not fear,
>> for there always is a sweet harmony between providences and
>>> promises.
> All day long you seek to bring your promises to fruition.

You are so greatly concerned, O Christ, about the welfare of your church and your people.
> You are more concerned than I am about the victory of love in the world.
> Elevate my concern about the faithfulness and prosperity of your church,
>> because my own peace is so closely bound to it.
>>> The peace of the church spills over into my life.
>>> I have committed the whole of who I am to this ship
>>>> and it has embarked on a voyage through treacherous seas.
> If the church is lost, then I am lost; farewell prosperity and all that I can call good.
> So wisely steer the course and carry the ship safely into its harbor.

The church and this world, O Christ, are laid upon your shoulders
> the scepter has been put into your hand,
> and all power both in heaven and earth has been committed to you.
>> You are my King, upon the holy hill of Zion.
>> You direct all your power—the power of love—toward
>>> the success of your mission in the world through the church.
>> I sit under the shadow of your wing in such peace and delight.
>> Amen.

—Samuel Annesley, *Sermons (Psalm 97:1–2)* [44]

## Hymn:

Rejoice, the Lord is King!
> Your Lord and King adore;

mortals, give thanks and sing,
> and triumph evermore.

## Praying in the Spirit of Christ

*Refrain*
Lift up your heart, lift up your voice;
rejoice; again I say, rejoice.

Jesus the Savior reigns,
    the God of truth and love;
when he had purged our stains,
    he took his seat above.
*Refrain*

His kingdom cannot fail;
    he rules o'er earth and heaven;
the keys of earth and hell
    are to our Jesus given.
*Refrain*

Rejoice in glorious hope!
    Jesus the Judge shall come,
and take his servants up
    to their eternal home.

*Refrain*

—*UMH* 715

# 44

## *Love Your Enemies*

**Scripture:**

I say to you, love your enemies and pray for those who harass you.

—Matthew 5:44

**Prayer:**

Grant me grace, O God, to love my enemies without malice or rancor
    proceeding from my resentment concerning the wounds I have
       sustained.
   If I fixate on the offences perpetrated against me,
      I will certainly nurture vindictiveness and revenge in my heart.
   I want to aim at a full and perfect reconciliation with others,
     and I need your Spirit to be able to pray genuinely for those
        who harass me.
   How can I expect your blessing if I hold onto resentment and anger?
   If I truly love my enemies I cannot permit my memory of wounds
     to fester and pollute my soul from the inside out.

## Praying in the Spirit of Christ

Grant me grace, O God, to relinquish my desire for revenge.
    If I return evil for evil, these actions bring me no genuine reparation.
    I want to cultivate true Christ-like love for my enemies in my heart
        and never want to willingly inflict pain or injury on anyone.
    How can I be pleased with the misery of others, no matter what they have done?
    If I truly love my enemies I must actually desire the best for them.
Grant me grace, O God, to acknowledge how often I have wounded others.
    Help me never to think of myself more highly than I ought;
        reveal to me the attitudes and actions that alienate me from others.
    The darker part of my nature can easily take pleasure in the fall of my enemies,
        as if I actually had taken revenge on them myself.
    How can I feast on love if my satisfaction comes from feeding my hate?
    If I truly love my enemies my heart must be filled with goodness, not pride.
Grant me grace, O God, to learn from Jesus, who was both gentle and humble.
    Chase disdain and contempt from my heart.
    Fill my heart with a love that is neither arrogant nor rude,
        that does not seek its own advantage,
            that does not keep a record of wrongs,
                but finds joy in the truth.
    Fill my heart with a love that puts up with all things, trusts in all things, hopes for all things, endures all things. Amen.

—Henry Scougal, *Discourses* [45]

**Hymn:**

Our earth we now lament to see
    with floods of wickedness overflowed,
with violence, wrong, and cruelty,
    one wide-extended field of blood,
where men, like fiends, each other tear
in all the hellish rage of war.

O might the universal Friend
    this havoc of his creatures see!
Bid our unnatural discord end,
    declare us reconciled in thee!
Write kindness on our inward parts,
and chase the murderer from our hearts!

*—UMH* 449

# 45

## *Servants of God*

**Scripture:**

Then the people answered, "God forbid that we ever leave the Lord to serve other gods!"

—Joshua 24:16

**Prayer:**

We give up ourselves, O God, our souls and bodies, entirely to you,
    uniting ourselves to you by the strongest bonds that we can.
    We resolve to be yours and only yours forever.
        Just as fire ascends upwards when that which keeps it down is removed
        we pray for you to break down every barrier between us
            so we can rise into your presence and serve you.

We are your children, O God, and you are the only source of our being and life.
> We acknowledge you as our only supporter, preserver, and maintainer in life.
> We draw our life from you as surely as the tree from its root.
>> You refresh us by heat and light, nourishing us with all good things;
>>> without you we would have nothing.

We believe that you save us, O God, through your only begotten Son.
> He delivers us from sin and death and brings us to everlasting life.
> We rejoice in the fact that you have taken possession of us by the Holy Spirit,
>> who works in us all the time to cultivate a servant spirit within us.
> When we were baptized, renouncing the devil, the world, and the flesh,
>> we gave up ourselves to you—Father, Son, and Holy Spirit.
> At the Table of the Lord we renew this commitment to you continually.
>> In the Holy Mystery we commemorate the greatest expression
>>> of the greatest love that has ever been seen and known.
>> There we offer and present ourselves—our souls and our bodies—
>>> as a reasonable, holy, and lively sacrifice to you.

We cannot ever hope to see you, O God, without the holiness you command.
> So we pray that you will make us holy, even as you are holy.
>> We cannot find any greater happiness than in serving you.
>> These three words—holiness, perfection, happiness—
>>> mean the same thing to us, and we pray expectantly for this.
>> We yearn to be perfect, completely holy, and entirely yours.
>> We want to be so united to you in our service
>>> that nothing can dissolve the union—blessed forevermore. Amen.

—*The Country Parson's Advice to His Parishioners* (Part 2) [45]

## Praying in the Spirit of Christ

**Hymn:**

Ye servants of God, your Master proclaim,
and publish abroad his wonderful name;
the name all-victorious of Jesus extol,
his kingdom is glorious and rules over all.

God ruleth on high, almighty to save,
and still he is nigh, his presence we have;
the great congregation his triumph shall sing,
ascribing salvation to Jesus, our King.

"Salvation to God, who sits on the throne!"
Let all cry aloud and honor the Son;
the praises of Jesus the angels proclaim,
fall down on their faces and worship the Lamb.

Then let us adore and give him his right,
all glory and power, all wisdom and might;
all honor and blessing with angels above,
and thanks never ceasing and infinite love.

*—UMH* 181

# 46

## *The Cross of Christ*

**Scripture:**

The message of the cross is foolishness to those who are being destroyed.
　But it is the power of God for those of us who are being saved.

　　　　　　　　　　　　　　　　　　　　—1 Corinthians 1:18

**Prayer:**

Through your cross, O blessed Jesus, you sought me,
　　you cured me, you delivered me, you liberated me, and you loved me.
　　So in the cross I will seek you, and there I will find you;
　　　　and having found you, you will help me.
　　　　You will deliver me from myself, since I so often turn
　　　　　　from the very love in which my salvation may be found.
　I am so ashamed and my heart breaks because you loved me so much
　　and I love you so little in return.
　　　I don't even deserve to be called your servant
　　　　　because I am so afraid to put on the clothing of true
　　　　　　discipleship.

## Praying in the Spirit of Christ

Tell me, O beloved Jesus, was there ever a day when you took off that robe of suffering
   in order to clothe yourself with the garments of repose and ease?
      O no! You were far from resting because you were always consumed with love,
         and it was this love that led you to suffer.
When they stripped you of your clothes, O blessed Jesus, to nail you upon the cross,
   your blood—the symbol of your great love—became your garment.
   Your head was crowned with thorns, your back was scourged by the whip,
      your hands were pierced with two nails, and your feet with another.
   You bore the punishment that makes me whole; by your wounds I am healed.
   How could any who behold you on the cross not fall in love with you
      with a love that answers your unbounded love?
   Seeing you in such a plight and freely offering your life for the life of the world,
      how could anything but love well up in my heart?
For my part, O blessed Jesus, I am resolved to hold onto you
   and love you with a perfect love.
   I know that my true happiness consists in being yours and in your being mine.
   I want to know you and you alone.
      You told me that if I remain in you, you will remain in me.
      A branch cannot produce fruit by itself, but must remain in the vine.
      My true joy consists in your being mine and in my being yours.
      You alone are my true good. Amen.

—Don Juan d'Avila, *Spiritual Letters* [46]

**Hymn:**

Behold the Savior of mankind
    nailed to the shameful tree;
how vast the love that Him inclined
    to bleed and die for thee!

Hark, how he groans, while nature shakes,
    and earth's strong pillars bend!
The temple's veil in sunder breaks,
    the solid marbles rend.

'Tis done! the precious ransom's paid!
    "Receive my soul!" he cries;
see where he bows his sacred head!
    He bows His head and dies!

But soon he'll break death's envious chain
    and in full glory shine,
O Lamb of God, was ever pain,
    was ever love like thine?

*—UMH 293*

# 47

## *The Work of Christ*

**Scripture:**

It's appropriate for us to have this kind of high priest: holy, innocent, incorrupt, separate from sinners, and raised high above the heavens.

—Hebrews 7:26

**Prayer:**

I believe, Lord Jesus, that you lived to God and died to sin,
>   that I might die to sin and live with you eternally.
>   By faith, I follow you from your Incarnation to your passion and death,
>> believing all that you did or suffered was for my sake.
>   Not only did you take my nature upon yourself,
>> you obeyed and suffered so that your active obedience,
>>> as well as your passion, was for me.

## The Work of Christ

I believe, Lord Jesus, that you fulfilled all the qualifications in their absolute perfection,
> to be my high priest, and made atonement for all the sins of the world.
> You are God—co-equal with the Father—and you acted
>> merely on my behalf and for my benefit.

I believe, Lord Jesus, that whatever you did or suffered in the flesh
> was meritorious for me.
>> Because of what you have done, I know that I am truly accepted.
>> You took my sins into your very being
>>> and carried that burden on my behalf.

I believe, Lord Jesus, that your death was infinitely more satisfactory
> to divine justice than if I had died to eternity.

Because of your death once for all, justice is actually and perfectly satisfied.
> I never could have died to my sin enough.
> Your death not only deals with the just condemnation
>> that my sin demands—it did not only pluck out its sting—
>> but your redemptive work deprives sin of its strength.
> Your death enables me to die to sin.
>> It breaks the power of sin.
>> It makes it possible for me to actually become righteous
>>> as I participate in you.
>> It restores your image in my life.

All I need to do is cry: "Mercy, mercy, O gracious Father."
> Your work has set me free. Amen.

—Bishop Beveridge, *Thoughts on Religion (Article 6)* [47]

## Praying in the Spirit of Christ

**Hymn:**

O Love divine, what hast thou done!
The immortal God hath died for me!
The Father's coeternal Son
bore all my sins upon the tree.
Th' immortal God for me hath died:
My Lord, my Love, is crucified!

Is crucified for me and you,
to bring us rebels back to God.
Believe, believe the record true,
ye all are bought with Jesus' blood.
Pardon for all flows from his side:
My Lord, my Love, is crucified!

—*UMH* 287:1–2

# 48

*Breathing God's Love*

**Scripture:**

So then let's also run the race that is laid out in front of us, since we have such a great cloud of witnesses surrounding us. Let's throw off any extra baggage, get rid of the sin that trips us up.

—Hebrews 12:1

**Prayer:**

We pray, O God, for the fullest measure of humility.
    We desire to be intimately united with you,
        to have a full knowledge of your greatness
            and our proper place in relation to you.
    We desire for everyone to know that you are God—you are everything.
    We desire for the rays of the your divine radiance
        to fall continually on our souls as those of the sun on a crystal
            mirror.
    Transform us into the image of Christ by an act of pure love.
    Purify our conscience through our intimate connection with you.

## Praying in the Spirit of Christ

We pray, O God, for the eradication of sin from our lives.
> Enable us to love you with all our whole being and with deep humility.
>> If we love you with all our heart and with all our mind,
>>> your love will indwell our lives and fill all our actions.
> Enable us to love our neighbors as we love ourselves.
>> If we abide in you and our union increases without hindrance,
>>> your love will freely overflow from our lives into the lives of others.

We pray, O God, for endurance through the inward and outward struggles in our lives.
> We offer all that we have suffered as a sacrifice to you.
> Open our hearts to receive you as a healing presence—
>> in our participation in the Supper of the Lord
>> and in our communion with your abiding love.

We pray, O God, for the church that it may increase and prosper.
> May our outward works reflect an inward piety of joy and thanksgiving.
> When we lift up our hearts to you, grant us your assistance and blessing.
> Help us to be living portraits of Jesus Christ—truly crucified with him and fully committed to your life in our souls.
>> Keep our eyes and our hearts fixed on Jesus,
>>> the pioneer and perfecter of our faith. Amen.

—*The Life of Gregory Lopez* [50]

**Hymn:**

Give me the faith which can remove
    and sink the mountain to a plain;
give me the childlike praying love,
    which longs to build thy house again;
thy love, let it my heart o'erpower,
and all my simple soul devour.

I would the precious time redeem,
    and longer live for this alone,
to spend and to be spent for them
    who have not yet my Savior known;
fully on these my mission prove,
and only breathe, to breathe thy love.

*—UMH* 650:1-2

# 49

## *Thirst for God*

**Scripture:**

Just like a deer that craves streams of water, my whole being craves you, God.

—Psalm 42:1

**Prayer:**

Just like a deer that craves streams of water, O God, so my whole being craves you.
 I long to take my soul, as it were, out of the quiver of the body
  and to dart it up to heaven.
 I thirst and hope for an intimate communion with you.
  You are the one who created my innermost parts.
  You knit me together while I was still in my mother's womb.
  I give thanks to you that I was marvelously set apart.
  Your works are wonderful—I know that very well.

Just like a deer that craves streams of water, O God, so my whole being
 pants for you.
 I can hear the deer braying after brooks of cool water.
 Sometimes I am melancholy and fearful—a panting creature.
 Everything that surrounds me is dry and my thirst becomes excessive.
 Water can be scarce, and so it is with my spiritual life as well.
 I am sometimes chased—even hunted—my soul thirsts,
 and the way you quench my thirst not only brings relief,
 but even redemption, that energy needed to carry on.
Just like a deer that craves streams of water, O God, so my whole being
 yearns for you.
 A brook can hardly quench the thirst of the exhausted deer.
 Deep rivers cannot assuage its thirst.
 Deluge my spirit in its quest for an intimate relationship with you;
 strengthen the sinews of my soul,
 elevate my affections to the heights of heaven.
 Turn panting grace into zeal—a flaming edge of affection
 and the ruddy complexion of the soul.
 Spark within me a burning coal just fetched from the altar.
 Draw me higher still:
 Grant that I may thirst for nothing less than the fullness of your
  love
 and enter into heaven panting, my thirst assuaged,
 immersed for all eternity in your glorious love.
 Amen.

—Nathaniel Culverwell, *The Panting Soul* [Supplement]

## Praying in the Spirit of Christ

**Hymn:**

Saints of God, your Savior praise,
    who the door hath opened wide;
he hath given the word of grace,
    Jesus' word is glorified;
Jesus mighty to redeem,
    who alone the work hath wrought;
worthy is the work of him,
    him who spake a world from naught.

Saw ye not the cloud arise,
    little as a human hand?
now it spreads along the skies,
    hangs o'er all the thirsty land.
Lo! the promise of a shower
    drops already from above;
but the Lord will shortly pour
    all the spirit of his love.

*—UMH* 541:3-4

# 50

## *A Fellowship of Love*

**Scripture:**

Our fellowship is with the Father and with his Son, Jesus Christ. We are writing these things so that our joy can be complete.

—1 John 1:4

**Prayer:**

We seek a fellowship with you, O Triune God, in which we harmonize in mutual love.
    Transport our souls into a binding friendship with you
        in which you drown all our personal interests in our communion with you.
    Dissolve our concerns for ours and yours;
        reveal to us how ours is yours and yours is ours;
            our hearts are yours and your honor is ours.

Shape our loves so that they conform to your great love for us and for the world.
> You so loved the world that you gave your only Son.
> Help us demonstrate your love by abandoning power and privilege
>> and by condescending, like Jesus, to take on the status of servants
>>> as the instruments of your mission of love in the world.

You have accepted us, O Triune God, into this blessed fellowship with you.
> As we experience a greater unity in love and service with you,
>> may we long for more unity among ourselves,
>>> for you are the uniting principle that binds us together.
> The closer we move toward you—the center point of our lives—
>> the closer we come to one another.

From the depths of our being, O Triune God, we seek your image.
> We desire to be conformed to that image.
> We see you in the face of Jesus.
> We have some sense of the infinite blessedness and perfection
>> that is found only in the source of our being.
> So our happiness or our misery depends upon this one thing—
>> that upon which our souls focus their attention.

We genuinely desire, O Triune God, to immerse ourselves in the fullness of your being,
> that which is eternally and universally good,
>> for we know that only you can grant our souls rest and tranquility,
>>> joy and satisfaction, the blessedness of abiding
>>>> in the object of our greatest love. Amen.

—Hugh Binning, *Fellowship with God* [Supplement]

**Hymn:**

Jesus, united by thy grace
   and each to each endeared,
with confidence we seek thy face
   and know our prayer is heard.

Up unto thee, our living Head,
   let us in all things grow;
till thou hast made us free indeed
   and spotless here below.

Touched by the lodestone of thy love,
   let all our hearts agree,
and ever toward each other move,
   and ever move toward thee.

To thee, inseparably joined,
   let all our spirits cleave;
O may we all the loving mind
   that was in thee receive.

*—UMH* 561:1, 3–5

# 51

## *Perfect Love*

**Scripture:**

You must love the Lord your God with all your heart, with all your being, with all your mind, and with all your strength.

—Mark 12:30

**Prayer:**

I want to love you, O God, with my whole heart.
>Nothing could be sweeter, more pleasant, more honorable.
>Forgive me for when I have loved riches, for they gave me abundance of trouble.
>Forgive me for when I loved the delights of this life,
>>for I found that all pleasure inevitably entailed some hidden pain.

## PERFECT LOVE

Forgive me for when I loved people with the kind of love I owed you,
> for it was always painful for me to please them,
>> and the fear of losing them was a continual anxiety to me.
>>> All other loves have grief mingled with their greatest pleasures.
>>> All earthly pleasures end in sadness.

I want to love you, O God, with my whole heart.
> You honor me by accepting the love I offer to you, no matter how imperfect.
> You delight in honoring me when I simply seek to love you.
> You rejoice in all my faltering efforts to love you with my whole heart—
>> to love you perfectly.

I want to love you, O God, with my whole heart.
> Grant me the grace to seek your perfect love,
>> and to resist the seductive powers of this world
>>> that make false claims upon my love.
> Grant me the grace to accept the love that you freely offer to me;
>> all you require is that I desire it and ask for it.
> Grant me the grace to triumph when an inward battle ensues
>> and my affections turn away from you and to myself—
>>> free me from a self-love that only leads to loss and pain.
> Grant me the grace to spare nothing to gain the treasure of your love.
>> Help me to put my faith into practice—to trust in you for all things;
>>> only you can liberate my heart to love you fully.
>> Help me to embrace your love as the authentic center of my very being. Amen.

—Antoinette Bourignon, *Solid Virtue* [Supplement]

## Praying in the Spirit of Christ

**Hymn:**

Come, Almighty to deliver,
    let us all thy life receive;
suddenly return and never,
    nevermore thy temples leave.
Thee we would be always blessing,
    serve thee as thy hosts above,
pray and praise thee without ceasing,
    glory in thy perfect love.

Finish, then, thy new creation;
    pure and spotless let us be.
Let us see thy great salvation
    perfectly restored in thee;
changed from glory into glory,
    till in heaven we take our place,
till we cast our crowns before thee,
    lost in wonder, love, and praise.

*—UMH 384:3-4*

# 52

## *Pure, Unbounded Love*

**Scripture:**

I ask that you'll know the love of Christ that is beyond knowledge so that you will be filled entirely with the fullness of God.

—Ephesians 3:19

**Prayer:**

We long to experience your pure, unbounded love, O God.
    We have no desire to understand anything other than your love.
    All your commandments have but one purpose:
        love flowing out of a heart rooted in you.
    We receive this gift of abundant life through faith in Christ Jesus;
        faith unites us to Christ and enables us to offer our lives to you;
        faith lifts our hearts up to you and you enter the depth of our
            being,
                making us one—a gracious inexplicable union.

## Praying in the Spirit of Christ

We long to dwell in your pure, unbounded love, O God.
> We yearn to be so inflamed with this love
>> that all his thoughts, words, and actions are the fruit of it;
>> that this love becomes the beginning and ending of everything we do;
>> that this fire in our hearts burns and consumes without ceasing.
>> that the flames of this divine fire burst forth for all to see.
>
> We yearn to cry out: "My God and my All!"

We long to be overcome by your pure, unbounded love, O God.
> We want to be all on fire with your love!
>> to stand in constant awe before your unbounded love;
>> to magnify the sight of your glorious majesty;
>> to revere your continual presence;
>> to extol your eternal greatness;
>> to adore you with our whole being.

We long to share your pure, unbounded love, O God.
> Use us as your instruments so that all people might come to know you and love you.
>
> Overwhelm us with your grace so that our souls might be filled with your love.
>
> May the holiness and humility—the love—that you form in our souls,
>> always point to your pure, unbounded love
>>> to your great glory, now and forevermore. Amen.

—*The Life of Monsieur de Renty* [Supplement]


**Hymn:**

'Tis Love! 'tis Love! Thou diedst for me,
   I hear thy whisper in my heart.
The morning breaks, the shadows flee,
   pure Universal Love thou art:
To me, to all, thy mercies move—
thy nature, and thy name is Love.

My prayer hath power with God; the grace
   unspeakable I now receive;
through faith I see thee face to face,
   I see thee face to face, and live!
In vain I have not wept and strove—
thy nature, and thy name is Love.

I know thee, Savior, who thou art,
   Jesus, the feeble sinner's friend;
nor wilt thou with the night depart,
   but stay and love me to the end:
thy mercies never shall remove,
thy nature, and thy name is Love.

                                  —*UMH* 387:9–11

## Contemporary Editions of Original Sources

All the devotional materials collected in this volume are excerpts from classics of spiritual devotion and Christian theology found in John Wesley's edition of these texts in the *Christian Library*, but modernized and translated here into the forms of prayer. Most of these sources are not accessible today in contemporary editions. Those editions listed below, numbered according to the devotion in which they appear, are both readily accessible and modernized versions of the classic texts.

1. Clement of Rome (d. 99). "First Epistle to the Corinthians." In *Early Christian Writings: The Apostolic Fathers*, edited by Andrew Louth. New York: Penguin, 1987. ISBN 978-0140444759.

2. Macarius of Egypt (c. 300–91). "Homilies." In *Pseudo-Macarius: The Fifty Spiritual Homilies and the Great Letter*, edited by George A. Maloney. Classics of Western Spirituality. Mahwah, NJ: Paulist, 1992. ISBN 978-0809133123.

3. Johann Arndt (1555–1621). *Johann Arndt: True Christianity*, edited by Peter Erb. Classics of Western Spirituality. Mahwah, NJ: Paulist, 1978. ISBN 978-0809121922.

4. John Foxe (1516–87). *Foxe's Book of Martyrs: Select Narratives*, edited by John King. Oxford World's Classics. New York: Oxford University Press, 2009. ISBN 978-0199236848.

13. Jeremy Taylor (1613–67). "Rules and Exercises of Holy Living." In *Jeremy Taylor: Selected Works*, edited by Thomas Carroll. Classics of Western Spirituality. Mahwah, NJ: Paulist, 1990. ISBN 978-0809131754.

CONTEMPORARY EDITIONS OF ORIGINAL SOURCES

21. Blaise Pascal (1623–62). *Blaise Pascal: Pensées,* translated by A. J. Krailsheimer. New York: Penguin, 1995. ISBN 978-0140446456.

36. Francois Fenelon (1651–1715). "Letters." In *Fenelon: Selected Writings,* edited by Chad Helms. Classics of Western Spirituality. Mahwah, NJ: Paulist, 2006. ISBN 978-0809141517.

37. & 38. Brother Lawrence (c. 1614–91). *The Practice of the Presence of God.* Translated by John J. Delaney. Garden City, NY: Image, 1977. ISBN 978-0385128612.

40. Miguel de Molinos (1628–96). *Miguel de Molinos: The Spiritual Guide.* Edited by Robert P. Baird. Classics of Western Spirituality. Mahwah, NJ: Paulist, 2010. ISBN 978-0809105830.

44. Henry Scougal (1650–78). "Discourses on Important Subjects." In *The Works of the Rev. H. Scougal.* Edited by George Garden. Rochester, NY: Scholars Choice, 2015. ISBN 978-1295938209.

45. *The Country Parson's Advice to His Parishioners.* Edited by George Byron Koch. New York: Monarch, 1998. ISBN 978-1854244079.

# Scripture Index of Devotion Texts

## The Old Testament (Hebrew Scriptures)

| Scripture Text | Devotion Number |
| --- | --- |
| Genesis 28:15 | 38 |
| Joshua 24:16 | 45 |
| Leviticus 6:13 | 20 |
| Psalm 24:7 | 43 |
| Psalm 37:4 | 17 |
| Psalm 42:1 | 49 |
| Psalm 46:1 | 32 |
| Psalm 51:10 | 39 |
| Psalm 145:9 | 12 |
| Ecclesiastes 9:10 | 31 |
| Isaiah 55:6 | 37 |
| Isaiah 60:1 | 30 |
| Jeremiah 29:11 | 25 |
| Ezekiel 18:32 | 29 |
| Micah 6:8 | 22 |

## The New Testament

| Scripture Text | Devotion Number |
| --- | --- |
| Matthew 5:44 | 44 |
| Matthew 11:28 | 36 |
| Mark 12:30 | 51 |

## Scripture Index of Devotion Texts

| Luke 10:27 | 7 |
| --- | --- |
| John 1:14 | 8 |
| John 8:36 | 41 |
| John 14:6 | 2 |
| John 17:21 | 24 |
| Acts 1:8 | 10 |
| Acts 2:46 | 27 |
| Acts 17:28 | 13 |
| Acts 24:16 | 34 |
| Romans 8:34 | 9 |
| Romans 11:36 | 1 |
| 1 Corinthians 1:18 | 46 |
| 1 Corinthians 11:23–25 | 23 |
| 1 Corinthians 13:7 | 16 |
| 1 Corinthians 15:55 | 42 |
| 2 Corinthians 4:6 | 21 |
| 2 Corinthians 5:17 | 3 |
| Galatians 5:6 | 6 |
| Galatians 5:25 | 26 |
| Ephesians 3:19 | 52 |
| Ephesians 4:2b-3 | 40 |
| Philippians 3:10 | 4 |
| Philippians 4:7 | 5 |
| Colossians 3:17 | 18 |
| 1 Thessalonians 5:17 | 19 |
| 1 John 1:4 | 50 |
| 1 John 1:5 | 14 |
| 1 John 4:16 | 11 |
| 1 John 5:3 | 15 |
| James 1:22 | 35 |
| Hebrews 4:1 | 33 |
| Hebrews 7:26 | 47 |
| Hebrews 12:1 | 48 |
| Revelation 3:20 | 28 |

# Index of Hymns

In the following index the hymn selections are placed in numerical sequence as they appear in *The United Methodist Hymnal*. The numbers following the colon indicate the stanzas of the hymn. If no stanzas are indicated, the hymn is reproduced in its entirety.

| Hymn | First Line | Devotion |
|---|---|---|
| 57:1–2, 7–8 | O for a thousand tongues to sing | 30 |
| 88:1, 4 | Maker, in whom we move | 13 |
| 96:1, 3 | Praise the Lord who reigns above | 1 |
| 153:1–2 | Thou hidden source of calm repose | 5 |
| 173:1, 3 | Christ, whose glory fills the skies | 14 |
| 181 | Ye servants of God | 45 |
| 183:1–2 | Jesu, thy boundless love to me | 3 |
| 183:3–4 | Jesu, thy boundless love to me | 32 |
| 193:3–6 | Jesus! The name high over all | 25 |
| 196 | Come, thou long-expected Jesus | 2 |
| 240:2–3 | Hark! The herald angels sing | 8 |
| 287:1–2 | O Love divine, what hast thou done | 47 |
| 293 | Behold the Savior of mankind | 46 |
| 302:1, 3–4, 6 | Christ the Lord is risen today | 44 |
| 312 | Hail the day that sees him rise | 9 |
| 332:1 & 4 | Spirit of faith, come down | 10 |
| 339:1–3, 5 | Come, sinners to the gospel feast | 27 |
| 346:1, 7 | Sinners, turn: why will you die | 29 |
| 363:1, 3–4 | And can it be that I should gain | 41 |
| 372:1–4 | How can we sinners know | 12 |

## Index of Hymns

| | | |
|---|---|---|
| 384:1–2 | Love divine, all loves excelling | 16 |
| 384:3–4 | Love divine, all loves excelling | 51 |
| 385 | Let us plead for faith alone | 6 |
| 387:9–11 | Come, O thou traveler unknown | 52 |
| 388 | O come and dwell in me | 34 |
| 410:1, 3 | I want a principle within | 17 |
| 414:1, 3 | Thou hidden love of God, whose height | 21 |
| 414:2, 5 | Thou hidden love of God, whose height | 22 |
| 417:1–4 | O, for a heart to praise my God | 39 |
| 422 | Jesus, thine all-victorous love | 11 |
| 438 | Forth in thy Name, O Lord, I go | 31 |
| 449 | Our earth we now lament to see | 44 |
| 479:1–2 | Jesus, lover of my soul | 36 |
| 479:3–4 | Jesus, lover of my soul | 7 |
| 501 | O Thou who camest from above | 20 |
| 513:3–4 | Soldiers of Christ, arise | 19 |
| 541:3–4 | See how great a flame aspires | 49 |
| 550:1–4 | Christ, from whom all blessing flow | 38 |
| 553:1–4 | And are we yet alive | 4 |
| 554:1–2, 4–5 | All praise to our redeeming Lord | 40 |
| 561:1, 3–5 | Jesus, united by thy grace | 50 |
| 562:2–5 | Jesus, Lord, we look to thee | 37 |
| 566:1–4 | Blest be the dear uniting love | 24 |
| 594 | Come, divine Interpreter | 15 |
| 603 | Come, Holy Ghost, our hearts inspire | 26 |
| 606:1–2 | Come, let us use the grace divine | 35 |
| 613 | O Thou who this mysterious bread | 28 |
| 627:1, 4 | O the depth of love divine | 23 |
| 650:1–2 | Give me the faith which can remove | 48 |
| 699 | Come, and let us sweetly join | 18 |
| 709:1, 4 | Come, let us join our friends above | 33 |
| 715 | Rejoice, the Lord is King | 43 |

www.ingramcontent.com/pod-product-compliance
Lightning Source LLC
Chambersburg PA
CBHW032152160426
43197CB00008B/884